Air Fryer Cookbook

*The Complete Air Fryer Cookbook
With Top 100+ Healthy Quick & Easy
Air Frying Recipes For Your Family
Everyday Meals*

By Linda C. Jones

Table of Contents

Introduction

First and foremost I would like to vehemently thank you for choosing this book about **Air Fryers**. But before we proceed I would like to know the category of persons you fall into.

Are you the type that does want to enjoy fried foods and still maintain yet a healthier version of your body? A type that is tired of wasting time and oil in the kitchen? A type that does want a clean and neat alternative to preparing his/her breakfast, lunch, and dinner each day? Or a type that searches for an easy-to-use kitchen gadget that can bake, grill, and fry in a matter of minutes? Well if you fall into any of this categories of people, then you are certainly at the right spot, as the Air Fryer is the best solution to virtually all the problems you have been facing in the kitchen. And by so doing this book will guide you on how to get the most out of the air fryer as it can save time, reinforce safety in the kitchen, and allow you to enjoy fried meals without any fear of an unhealthy aftermath in the body.

This book will also act as a guide on how to prepare some of your favorite meals that will not only be healthy but also packed with texture and flavor. Now most of us might be thinking that air fryers are limited to cooking only, but in reality it is a multipurpose device as it can fry, roast, grill, and bake delicious, mouth-watery meals. And as such this book offers a various set of recipes ranging from breakfast, lunch, dinner, appetizers, side dishes, and desserts, which above all are easy to prepare just by using this kitchen appliance(Air Fryers).

Before embarking on this air frying recipes, you will get to know more about the air fryer itself as an appliance and the secrets behind it. It is a complete guide for your Air Fryer Cooking! With all that said, once again thank you for reading this book, I hope that you will get the best out of it!

Chapter 1: Everything About the Air Fryer

The air fryer is a modern kitchen gadget that uses the rapid circulation of hot air to cook foods through. If you are looking for healthy meals that are rich in texture, packed with flavor, nutrients, and low in fat, then using an air fryer would be the best choice. In this chapter, you will get to learn everything you need to know about air frying and how to use it as a professional.

What is An Air Fryer?

An air fryer is a one-of-a-kind conventional form of oven, almost the same size as a rice cooker. Cooking with an air fryer utilizes the rapid circulation of hot air around your meals (as the picture shows below). The circulation of heat moves at an incredibly high speed that it cooks quickly providing a crispy texture on the outside and a soft one the inside. Air fryers can fry, bake, roast, and grill any sorts of foods with the requirement of little to no oil at all.

Also, the air fryers have a timer and an adjustable temperature manager which means that you do not need to keep a tab on your food as everything is done automatically. Using an air fryer is a matter of adding the meal, adjusting the temperature, and setting the time. Although some recipes may require a little extra care, other than that, it's most often a times a pretty much smooth sailing experience whenever it comes to using the air fryers.

The Benefits of The Air Fryers

There is an endless list of benefits when it comes to air frying, and below are some of them:

1. Air fryers can provide you with delicious and tasty meals every day at any time.

2. Air fryers avoid dry fried foods (common in deep fryers), while at the same time retains the crispy texture on the outside.

3. Air fryers can cook and heat foods in a matter of minutes.

4. Air fryers is multiple purpose kitchen device as it can fry, grill, roast, bake, and even make soups.

5. Air fryers are user-friendly appliance that comes with a timer, which means that you can cook your food and walk away without any fear of oil splattering or spillages, grease fires, burning, or foods sticking.

6. Air fryers saves money as you will be using lesser oil to fry foods.

7. Air fryers are low-maintenance and easily cleaned devices as most parts can be stripped and dish washed.

8. Air fryers can prepare foods with eighty percent less fat than oil fried foods, thus making it much healthier.

9. Air fryers contains a lid for frying which makes it one of the safest devices that everyone could use in frying.

Air Fryer vs. Traditional Fryer

The major discrepancies between the traditional and air fryers include:

The Oil Factor: With an air fryer, it requires little to no oil, or in rare cases only a tablespoon or two at most cases, while on the other hand, deep fryers need a lot of oil. A deep fryer typically requires 1 to 4 quarts of cooking oil which also requires a constant oil replacement at certain intervals, meaning that you will spending more money on oil.

The Health Factor: With an air fryer, you will be using an unnoticeable percentage of oil, thus making it much healthier by reducing the fat content to 80 percent other than in the case of using a deep fryer.

The Neatness Factor: Air fryers have a dishwasher safe removable cooking component and is also easy to clean up. All that is required with an air fryer is to clean the cooking basket, cooking pan, and the drip pan which can all easily done by hand.

But in the case of using the deep fryers, oil vapors can settle on the counter top, kitchen walls, and even the floors, making it messy and detrimental to ones health. Thus, you will spend more time cleaning these surfaces. Also, cleaning the deep fryer is not easy, depending on the brand, some parts may or may not be safe to dish wash, and some areas may be impossible to reach.

The Safety Factor: Air frying is safe to use, because your cooking will be done while the food is covered with a lid. It can prepare foods without the need for you to stand beside it. However, when using a deep fryer, you need to stand in front of the hot oil to cook. Using the deep fryer carries more risk as the oil can splatter making the floors slippery, flickering on your skin, and even grease fire. Foods can also get burnt in the hot oil whereas with an air fryer you will just need to set the temperature, timer and walk away.

The Versatility Factor: Air fryers have multiple uses compared to the deep fryers. You can fry, grill, roast, and bake in your air fryers whereas you can use only deep fries in a deep fryer.

The Taste Factor: Deep fryers have a crunchier texture compared to the air fryers, because deep fryers are suitable for wet battered foods. In an air fryer, using wet batter foods will make the batter splatter, implying that to obtain a more crunchier texture, you will need to add an additional tablespoon of oil to your meals using an air fryer. The only difference would be the degree of crunchiness of the skin and of course the fat content.

The Time Factor: Deep frying is quicker than air frying. With deep fryers, heat is rapidly transferred from the hot oil to the food items. French fries will take around 10 to 15 minutes in your air fryer but only a couple of minutes in your deep fryer.

The Capacity Factor: Deep fryers generally have a large capacity than air fryers. If you are the type that cooks in large quantities (6+ servings), then deep fryers should be your most preferable. Air fryers is suitable for 2 to 4 servings at most.

The Reheating Factor: You can reheat foods in your air fryer in a matter of minutes compared to deep fryers. With deep fryers, it would not be so practical,because you will need to undergo the process of preparing the oil and cleaning afterward for just a small portion of food. Air fryers are more convenient and practical for reheating.

The Cost Factor: Air fryers are more costly than the deep fryers ranging from $50 to under $200 for the more expensive models. The air fryers cost more with most of the brands ranging from $100 to $200.

The Various Air Fryer Brands

Here is a list of some air fryer brands in the market. Find out which one is the best for you:

Phillips XL Air fryer: This air fryer has a large capacity making it a perfect choice for families or anyone who wishes to fry huge batches at once. This air fryer brand is also good for roasting, baking, and steaming ingredients. It comes with a dishwasher-safe for a smooth clean-up, a touch-screen interface, an adjustable temperature up to 390 degrees, and a 60-minute timer.

GoWISE USA GW22621 Electric Air Fryer: This brand has an adjustable temperature range of 175 to 390 degrees and can cook meals under 30 minutes. This air fryer is a practical choice for smaller families or for anyone who doesn't cook large batches frequently. The touchscreen is simple and has seven inbuilt programs. You can pick from the general food items including chips, chicken, fish, fries, and meat.

Power Air Fryer XL: This air fryer uses cyclonic heated air which cooks foods precisely and evenly for a delicious savory result without using any added oil. Other than that it comprises of an automated touch screen, and seven presets for popular meal items including chicken, fries, steaks, and baking goods.

Avalon Bay Digital Air Fryer: This brand comes with a fan that removes excess fats and oils from the food before air frying. The circulated air is then moved at a high speed to cook and heat the food efficiently for an even result. Also, this air fryer is perfect for baking, roasting, and grilling food items. The temperature for this brand ranges from 200 to 400 degrees and some customers claim you can use wet-battered ingredients with no expected splattering effects. It also has a non-slip rubber pad to hold the air fryer firmly in place.

NuWave Brio Air Fryer: This air fryer is good for cooking foods faster and simpler. This brand comes with of a preheat function, which brings the fryer to the best possible cooking temperature for your foods. It also has a digital touch screen to adjust the temperature and time.

Also in this brand to ensure safety, the air frying process won't begin until the fry bucket is fully locked.

How to Use an Air Fryer

There are 4 steps in using an air fryer, follow this set of instructions when cooking anything with it:

Preparation: To prevent ingredients from sticking to the air fryer basket, spray it with a nonstick cooking spray or add a tablespoon of oil. Don't over pack foods in your air fryer basket otherwise some parts won't be fully cooked thoroughly. If you are working with a marinated or wet ingredients, make sure you rub them dry, because this will help avert splattering or excess smoke.

Pre-Heating: Plug in your air fryer and preheat it.This usually takes around five minutes, although preheating is not that necessary,nevertheless it can reduce your time in cooking.

Cooking: If you are cooking frozen foods or items with small ingredients, try shaking the air fryer many times to prepare it evenly and efficiently. Also when cooking high fatty foods, you should have it at the back of your mind that ,the fats will drop to the base of the air fryer, which will thereafter need cleaning.

Cleaning: To ensure your air fryer stays in shape, make sure you clean it properly by purifying the air fryer basket and the pan after using them. Most air fryers come with dishwasher safe parts which makes this process easy.

How to Clean & Maintain An Air Fryer

The first thing you should have at your finger tips is that, if you do not clean and maintain your air fryer from time to time, it won't last long. Following these guidelines will secure the fact that your air fryer will remain effective and durable for years to come.

How to clean your air fryer

Unplug your air fryer from the wall socket and allow it to cool until you can touch.

Using a wet rag, wipe the exterior part of your air fryer.

Remove the air fryer pan, tray,basket and wash it with hot water and a dishwasher soap in your sink. These parts are removable and are safe for an easy cleanup.

Use a cloth or sponge to wipe and clean the inner part of your air fryer.

If you find any ingredients sticking in your air fryer, scrub it off with a brush.

Before adding the pan, tray, and basket back into your air fryer ensure they are entirely dry.

Once your air fryer is cleaned, store it safely.

How to maintain your air fryer

Your air fryer requires a standard form of maintenance to ensure it does not get damaged or work erroneously. To do this, one needs to follow this instructions:

Before using your air fryer, make sure you check the cord. That is, do not plug a damaged cord into an outlet; this can result in a ghastly injury or even death.

Make sure your air fryer is clean and free of any debris before you begin cooking. Check the inner part and make sure you remove anything redundant in there.

Ensure the air fryer is placed upright, on a flat surface.

Make sure that your air fryer is not too close to the wall or another appliance. Air fryers require 4-inches of space all around them.

One after the other, check each component of your air fryer, including the basket, pan, and handle.

If you find anything damaged or wrong with your air fryer, reach the manufacturer and get it replaced.

How to Choose a Good Air Fryer

There are wide varieties of air fryers available to you. The smartest choice will be to purchase from popular brands like Phillips, Kalorik, or some special air fryer brands recommended by experts and professionals. Here is some more insight when it comes to ordering your air fryer.

What affects the buyer's decision of your air fryer?

The increasing revenue of air fryers has reaped from its benefits of making healthy and low-cholesterol meals. With this you can cook fried chicken and potato chips that are healthy, nutritious, and less toxic than those of traditionally fried foods. Other benefits of air frying include fast cooking and an easy to use interface that it presents in your kitchen. With all this, who wouldn't buy an air fryer?

Tips on how to choose the air fryer best for you.

When it comes to owning an air fryer, there are some things you should have in in mind:

The size of your air fryer: The perfect sized air fryer gives your kitchen an enough space to serve, cook, and eat. To figure out the right size, you should have in mind that the ordinary air fryer can accommodate around 1.5 to 2 pounds of food items.

The capacity of your air fryer: Air fryers are electrically operated. Hence, inconsistencies in wattage stock can spark damage and electric shocks in your kitchen. Most standard ranges of air fryer capacity are from 700 to 1500 watts.

Controlling and signaling points: A good air fryer should have a digital touchscreen interface that can adjust temperature and time as well as switch modes. A timer is required to ensure fast and safe cooking. Some additional features should be checked for as it is going to give more comfort throughout your day to day cooking.

Warranty: Like any other device, buying gadgets will be more valuable due to its concentrated and considerate warranty terms. Having a warranty on your air fryer will be better than buying an air fryer without one. It is also preferable to purchase air fryers with full package home delivery.

The cost of your air fryer: Though an air fryer is highly recommended, it is costly compared to other kitchen gadgets. This is because of its level of utility as it prevents any form of grease fires, burns, and injury. The cost of air fryers is the most challenging factor for many and as such it is advisable that you should choose types that will lie within the whims and caprices of your budget.

It is also important to know that no matter the brand or price, all air fryers perform the same task irrespective. They all follow the principle of circulating hot air to cook and heat foods together. And so, your choice of an air fryer should not depend on technology or functions, but on the points mentioned above. Quality air fryers last longer and serve your needs better than investing in a cheaper module.

Where to Buy a Good Air Fryer?

There are many ways you can purchase an air fryer. Once you decide on the brand, you can Google and search up their websites. Alternatively, you can purchase air fryers on Amazon, online stores, and even grocery stores in their kitchen appliances section.

Air Frying Compatible Foods

Here is a list of compatible Air Frying foods:

Frozen Foods: Any kind of frozen foodstuff intended for baking purposes is a perfect fit for the air fryer. frozen things like fries, nuggets, and fish sticks cooks faster in your air fryer compared to your oven. And since there is no oil involved, it will lead to a low calories meal. For instance, French fries take around 12 minutes to achieve the crispy texture on the outside and a soft texture on the inside. You can shake the foods halfway through to ensure proper cooking and browning.

Raw Meat: You can roast any sort of meat in your air fryer, whether chicken, steak, pork, lamb, etc. A whole chicken will typically take about half an hour at 360 degrees F. to get done.

Vegetables: You can cook almost all forms of vegetables in your air fryer. Vegetables that you would normally grill can be done in your air fryer, and these includes cauliflower, green beans, onions, bell peppers can be all grilled in your air fryer.

Baked Goods: You can buy a nonstick baking dish along with your air fryer which is very useful when it comes to baking muffins, bread, lasagna, quiche, small cakes, or any other baked goods. This means you can bake anything you usually do in your oven using your air fryer with a more quicker and effective experience.

Roasting Nuts: Roasting nuts such as peanuts, walnuts, almonds, or any other kind of nuts can be easily done in your air fryer. This process will only take about 5 to 8 minutes, without it getting burned.

Wet-Battered Foods: Wet battered food is not suitable for air frying. The reason behind this is because the fast-moving air will burst the batter away from the food, causing it to splatter all over the cook basket,and creating a huge mess.

FAQs of Air Fryer

1. Can we cook various kinds of food in the air fryer?

Yes, you can easily prepare and cook any variety of foods in your air fryer. You can easily cook meats, potatoes, poultry, onion rings, and chicken nuggets .Aside from these things you can also bake cupcakes and grill vegetables.

2. How long does it take to cook frozen foods?

One of the great things about air frying frozen food is that it allows you to use the handle. But it usually takes more time to cook frozen foods compared to fresh ingredients.

3. How much can I cook in my air fryer?

This answer depends on the capacity of your air fryer. The majority of air fryers can hold up to 500 grams of food items. You can also see the max line of the basket on the air fryer which implies that the air fryer can be loaded up to that line.

4. Is there any specific kind of oils needed for air frying?

No, you don't need any special kind of oil for air frying. At most some recipes require a tablespoon or two of oil, of which you can use olive oil, coconut oil, vegetable oil, or butter spray.

5. Can I add more ingredients while the food is getting cooked in my air fryer?

Yes, you can add more ingredients while the food is getting cooked in your air fryer. However, be sure that the ingredients are added in the right away or else you may lose the heat which will result in an increase in the to cooking time.

6. Can I use a baking paper or aluminum foil in my air fryer?

Yes, you can use baking paper or aluminum foil, but you need to allocate some breathing space so that the steam can flow smoothly.

7. Is preheating required before I cook?

No, there is no need to preheat your air fryer. However, if you decide to preheat, it will take around 3 to 4 minutes and can help reduce the cooking time.

Now that we have known everything about the air fryer, let's cook some tasty and easy-to-make meals. It's effortless, all you have to do is just to follow the instructions properly. Also, do keep in mind that you are free to adjust the the recipes to your liking.

Chapter 2: Air Fryer Breakfast Recipes

1. Delicious Breakfast Souffle

Time: 20 minutes

Yield: 4

Ingredients:

- 6 eggs
- 1/3 of cup of milk
- ½ cup of shredded mozzarella cheese
- 1 tablespoon of freshly chopped parsley
- ½ cup of chopped ham
- 1 teaspoon of salt
- 1 teaspoon of black pepper
- ½ teaspoon of garlic powder

Instructions:

1. Grease 4 ramekins with a nonstick cooking spray.
2. Preheat your air fryer to 350 degrees Fahrenheit.
3. Using a large bowl, add and stir all the ingredients until it mixes properly.
4. Pour the egg mixture into the greased ramekins and place it inside your air fryer.
5. Cook it inside your air fryer for 8 minutes.
6. Then carefully remove the souffle from your air fryer and allow it to cool off.
7. Serve and enjoy!

Nutritional Information per serving:

Calories: 195, Fat: 15g, Protein: 9g, Carbohydrates: 6g, Dietary Fiber: 0.1g

2. Yummy Breakfast Italian Frittata

Time: 15 minutes

Yield: 4

Ingredients:

- 6 eggs
- 1/3 cup of milk
- 4-ounces of chopped Italian sausage
- 3 cups of stemmed and roughly chopped kale
- 1 red deseeded and chopped bell pepper
- ½ cup of a grated feta cheese
- 1 chopped zucchini
- 1 tablespoon of freshly chopped basil
- 1 teaspoon of garlic powder
- 1 teaspoon of onion powder
- 1 teaspoon of salt
- 1 teaspoon of black pepper

Instructions:

1. Preheat your air fryer to 360 degrees Fahrenheit.
2. Grease the air fryer pan with a nonstick cooking spray.
3. Add the Italian sausage to the pan and cook it inside your air fryer for 5 minutes.
4. While doing that, add and stir in the remaining ingredients until it mixes properly.
5. Add the egg mixture to the pan and allow it to cook inside your air fryer for 5 minutes.
6. Thereafter carefully remove the pan and allow it to cool off until it gets chill enough to serve.
7. Serve and enjoy!

Nutritional Information per serving:

Calories: 225, Fat: 14g, Protein: 20g, Dietary Fiber: 0.8g, Carbohydrates: 4.5g

3. Delectable Sweet Potato Hash Browns

Time: 20 minutes

Yield: 2

Ingredients:

- 2 grated sweet potatoes
- 3 eggs
- 1 cup of all-purpose flour
- 1 teaspoon of salt
- 1 teaspoon of black pepper
- 1 teaspoon of garlic powder
- 1 teaspoon of onion powder
- ½ teaspoon of nutmeg

Instructions:

1. Preheat your air fryer to 390 degrees Fahrenheit.
2. Using a bowl, add and mix all the ingredients using your washed hands.
3. Grease your air fryer pan with a nonstick cooking spray and stir the potato mixture using a spoon into patties.
4. If you have any leftovers, then cook it in batches. Place it inside your air fryer and cook for 15 minutes.
5. Serve and enjoy!

Nutritional Information per serving:

Calories: 135, Fat: 0.5g, Protein: 2.1g, Carbohydrates: 31g, Dietary Fiber: 4g

4. Good-Old Fashioned Pancakes

Time: 10 minutes

Yield: 1

Ingredients:

- 1 cup of all-purpose flour
- ½ cup of coconut flour
- 2 teaspoons of baking soda
- 1 1/2 teaspoon of baking powder
- 1 tablespoon of sugar
- 1 ¼ cup of milk
- 2 eggs
- 2 tablespoons of melted butter

Instructions:

1. Preheat your air fryer to 390 degrees Fahrenheit.
2. Using a large bowl, add and stir all the ingredients until it mixes properly.
3. Then grease your air fryer baking pan with a nonstick cooking spray or grease a safe heat dish with a nonstick cooking spray.
4. Add and spread the pancake dough proportionally and ensure there are no spaces in between. At this point you may need to cook in batches.
5. Place it inside your air fryer and cook for 10 minutes.
6. Thereafter, carefully remove the pancakes from your air fryer and repeat if you have any remaining batter.
7. Serve and enjoy!

Nutritional Information per serving:

Calories: 135, Fat: 3.4g, Dietary Fiber: 0.6g, Carbohydrates: 22g, Protein: 5g

5. Famous Bacon Breakfast Pie

Time: 25 minutes

Yield: 4

Ingredients:

- 1 already made thin pastry crust
- 4 eggs
- 2 cups of milk
- 3 sliced green onions
- 1 cup of shredded cheddar cheese
- 6 cooked and crumbled bacon
- 1 cooked and chopped potato
- 1 teaspoon of salt
- 1 teaspoon of black pepper
- 1 tablespoon of maple syrup

Instructions:

1. Preheat your air fryer to 390 degrees Fahrenheit.
2. Using your air fryer baking pan, press the pastry crust to fit in and cut off any extra edges on the sides.
3. Then using a large bowl, mix the eggs, milk, green onions, cheese, bacon bits, potato, salt, black pepper properly.
4. Pour the mixture over the pastry, cover it with aluminum foil, and poke the vent holes.
5. Place it inside your air fryer and bake it for 10 minutes or until it is done.
6. Thereafter, carefully remove the pie from your air fryer and allow it to cool off.
7. Serve and enjoy!

Nutritional Information per serving:

Calories: 170, Fat: 5g, Protein: 12g, Dietary Fiber: 1.6g, Carbohydrates: 22.8g

6. Must-Try Breakfast Blueberry Muffin

Time: 15 minutes

Yield: 2

Ingredients:

- 2 cups of rice flour
- 2 teaspoons of baking soda
- ½ teaspoon of salt
- 1 cup of sugar
- ½ cup of softened butter
- 2 eggs
- 1 cup of sugar
- 1 teaspoon of vanilla extract
- ½ cup of milk
- 1 cup of blueberries

Instructions:

1. Preheat your air fryer to 390 degrees Fahrenheit.
2. Using a large bowl, add and stir all the ingredients until it mixes properly.
3. Grease the muffin cups with a nonstick cooking spray or line it with a parchment paper. Pour the batter proportionally into each muffin cup.
4. Place it inside your air fryer and bake it for 10 minutes.
5. Thereafter, carefully remove it from your air fryer and allow it to chill.
6. Serve and enjoy!

Nutritional Information per serving:

Calories: 385, Fat: 9g, Protein: 7g, Carbohydrates: 50g, Dietary fiber: 3g

7. Classic Grilled Cheese

Time: 15 minutes

Yield: 2

Ingredients:

- 1 cup of shredded cheddar cheese
- ½ cup of melted butter
- 4 slices of bread

Instructions:

1. Preheat your air fryer to 360 degrees Fahrenheit.
2. Using two bowls, add the cheddar cheese to the first bowl and the melted butter to the second bowl.
3. Brush the butter on each side of all the bread pieces.
4. Add a ½ cup of cheese on the 2 pieces of bread, place the other slice of bread on top and put it inside your basket.
5. Allow it to cook for 5 minutes or until it has golden brown color, and the cheese has completely melted.
6. Thereafter, carefully remove it from your air fryer and allow it to cool.
7. Serve and enjoy!

Nutritional Information per serving:

Calories: 290, Fat: 15g, Protein: 9g, Carbohydrates: 28g, Dietary Fiber: 1.3g

8. Fabulous French Toast Sticks

Time: 20 minutes

Yield: 4

Ingredients:

- 4 eggs
- 1 cup of milk
- 6 slices of bread
- 2 tablespoons of sugar
- 1 teaspoon of vanilla extract
- 1 teaspoon of cinnamon
- ½ teaspoon of grated nutmeg
- 4 tablespoons of softened butter
- 1 cup of crushed cornflakes
- Maple syrup (for serving)

Instructions:

1. Preheat your air fryer to 360 degrees Fahrenheit.
2. Using a bowl, add and mix the eggs, milk, sugar, vanilla extract, cinnamon, and the nutmeg.
3. Cut the bread slices into 1-inch strips and brush the butter on each side.
4. Deepen each bread strips into the egg mixture and take off any excess.
5. Working in batches, place the bread slices into your air fryer and ensure you leave some spaces in between.
6. Cook it inside your air fryer for 6 minutes.
7. Then after 6 minutes, flip the bread sticks and cook it for an additional 4 minutes or until it has a golden brown color.
8. Thereafter, carefully remove the French toast strips and repeat if necessary.
9. Serve and enjoy alongside the maple syrup.

Nutritional Information per serving:

Calories: 370, Fat: 20g, Carbohydrates: 45g, Dietary Fiber: 1.5g, Protein: 6.7g

9. Savory Cheese and Bacon Muffins

Time: 22 minutes

Yield: 4

Ingredients:

- 1 ½ cup of all-purpose flour
- 2 teaspoons of baking powder
- ½ cup of milk
- 2 eggs
- 1 tablespoon of freshly chopped parsley
- 4 cooked and chopped bacon slices
- 1 thinly chopped onion
- ½ cup of shredded cheddar cheese
- ½ teaspoon of onion powder
- 1 teaspoon of salt
- 1 teaspoon of black pepper

Instructions:

1. Preheat your air fryer to 360 degrees Fahrenheit.
2. Using a large bowl, add and stir all the ingredients until it mixes properly.
3. Then grease the muffin cups with a nonstick cooking spray or line it with a parchment paper. Pour the batter proportionally into each muffin cup.
4. Place it inside your air fryer and bake it for 15 minutes.
5. Thereafter, carefully remove it from your air fryer and allow it to chill.

6. Serve and enjoy!

Nutritional Information per serving:

Calories: 180, Fat: 18g, Protein: 15g, Dietary Fiber: 0.7g, Carbohydrates: 16g

10. Best Air-Fried English Breakfast

Time: 25 minutes

Yield: 4

Ingredients:

- 8 sausages
- 8 bacon slices
- 4 eggs
- 1 (16-ounce) can of baked beans
- 8 slices of toast

Instructions:

1. Add the sausages and bacon slices to your air fryer and cook them for 10 minutes at a 320 degrees Fahrenheit.
2. Using a ramekin or heat-safe bowl, add the baked beans, then place another ramekin and add the eggs and whisk.
3. Increase the temperature to 290 degrees Fahrenheit.
4. Place it inside your air fryer and cook it for an additional 10 minutes or until everything is done.
5. Serve and enjoy!

Nutritional Information per serving:

Calories: 850, Fat: 40g, Protein: 48g, Dietary Fiber: 18g,

Carbohydrates: 20g

Chapter 3: Air Fryer Lunch Recipes

11. Delicious Air Fryer Roasted Stuffed Bell Peppers

Time: 25 minutes

Yield: 2

Ingredients:

- 2 medium stemmed and deseeded bell peppers, boiled for three minutes
- 1 cup of chopped red onion
- 2 minced garlic cloves
- 1 teaspoon of melted coconut oil
- 1 teaspoon of Worcestershire sauce
- 8-ounces of ground beef
- 2-ounces of shredded cheddar cheese
- 2-ounces of shredded mozzarella cheese
- ½ cup of tomato sauce
- 1 teaspoon of paprika
- 1 teaspoon of salt
- 1 teaspoon of black pepper

Instructions:

1. Preheat your air fryer to 390 degrees Fahrenheit.
2. Using a nonstick cooking pan, heat the coconut oil under average heat temperature until it gets melted.
3. Add the chopped red onions, garlic cloves and cook it until it starts producing some aroma, while still stirring from time to time.

4. Using a large bowl, add and mix the ground beef, onion, garlic cloves, half of the tomato sauce, waterside sauce, paprika, salt, and the black pepper properly.
5. Equally stuff the bell peppers with the ground beef mixture and top it with the leftover tomato sauce and cheese.
6. Place the stuffed bell peppers in your air fryer and cook it for 15 to 20 minutes or until the ground beef gets done.
7. Thereafter, carefully remove the bell peppers from your air fryer and allow it to cool.
8. Serve and enjoy!

Nutritional Information per serving:

Calories: 345, Fat: 9g, Protein: 19g, Dietary Fiber: 1g,

Carbohydrates: 27g

12. Incredible Air-Fried Burgers

Time: 45 minutes

Yield: 4

Ingredients:

- 1 pound of lean ground beef
- 1 teaspoon of salt
- 1 teaspoon of black pepper
- 1 teaspoon of onion powder
- 1 teaspoon of garlic powder
- 1 tablespoon of freshly chopped or dried parsley
- 1 tablespoon of Worcestershire sauce

Instructions:

1. Preheat your air fryer to 390 degrees Fahrenheit.
2. Using a large bowl, add and mix all the ingredients until it is properly mixed.
3. Grease your air fryer cooking tray with a nonstick cooking spray.
4. Segment the ground beef mixture into four medium-sized patties and place it in the tray.
5. Place the tray inside your air fryer and cook it for 25 minutes.
6. After 25 minutes, flip the burgers and cook it for an additional 20 minutes.
7. Then gather your burgers and add any toppings you like.
8. Serve and enjoy!

Nutritional Information per serving:

Calories: 148, Fat: 5g, Protein: 24g, Dietary Fiber: 0.3g,

Carbohydrates: 1.7g

13. Extraordinary Stuffed Zucchini with Bacon and Jalapeno

Time: 15 minutes

Yield: 2

Ingredients:

- 3 zucchinis
- 6 cooked and crumbled bacon slices
- 1 chopped jalapeno
- 2 chopped tomatoes
- 1 (8-ounce) can of tomato sauce
- 1 cup of shredded mozzarella cheese
- 1 tablespoon of freshly chopped parsley

- 1 teaspoon of salt
- 1 teaspoon of black pepper

Instructions:

1. Cut the zucchini vertically and scoop out the inner portions.
2. Using a large bowl, add and mix the bacon, jalapeno, salt, black pepper,the parsley properly.
3. Pour in the tomatoes, the tomato sauce and stir until it mixes properly.
4. Fill the zucchini with the ground beef mixture and sprinkle it with the cheese
5. Place the stuffed zucchini in your air fryer basket and cook it for 10 minutes.
6. Serve and enjoy!

Nutritional Information per serving:

Calories: 210, Fat: 8g, Protein: 23g, Dietary Fiber: 2g,

Carbohydrates: 6g

14. Good-Tasting Turkey Rolls

Time: 40 minutes

Yield: 4

Ingredients:

- 2 tortilla wraps
- 2 cups of shredded leftover turkey breast
- 2 eggs
- 1 tablespoon of honey
- 1 tablespoon of soy sauce

- 1 tablespoon of Chinese five-spice
- 1 teaspoon of Worcester sauce
- 1 teaspoon of salt
- 1 teaspoon of black pepper

Instructions:

1. Using a bowl, add the shredded leftover turkey breasts and seasonings. Mix it with your washed hands until it mixes properly.
2. Roll out the tortilla wraps thinly and avoid breaking or cracking any tortillas.
3. Using a bowl, add and beat the eggs.
4. Brush the egg wash on both sides and allow it to refrigerate for 30 minutes.
5. After thirty minutes, remove the tortilla wraps and cut it into 8 spring roll sheets.
6. Fill the shredded leftover turkey into each sheet.
7. Roll each turkey into a spring roll and brush it with the egg wash.
8. Place it inside your air fryer and cook it for 5 minutes at a 360 degrees Fahrenheit.

Nutritional Information per serving:

Calories: 45, Fat: 2g, Protein: 5g, Dietary Fiber: 0g,

Carbohydrates: 0.2g

15. Gratifying Stuffed Pizza Pastries

Time: 25 minutes

Yield: 2

Ingredients:

- 1 (13.5-ounce) package of refrigerated pizza crust
- 1 tablespoon of melted butter
- 1 teaspoon of Italian seasoning
- 1 teaspoon of garlic powder
- 1 teaspoon of salt
- 1 teaspoon of black pepper
- 3 tablespoons of grated Parmesan cheese
- 12-ounces of shredded mozzarella cheese
- 6-ounces of sliced pepperoni

Instructions:

1. Preheat your air fryer to 390 degrees Fahrenheit.
2. Grease a baking dish or your air fryer with a non-stick cooking spray.
3. Using a bowl, add and mix the melted butter, Italian seasoning, garlic powder, salt, and the black pepper.
4. Unroll the pizza into a surface and cut it into 12x8-inch rectangles which should be 24 squares in total.
5. For each square add a slice of pepperoni and cheese into the center.
6. Bring together the sides of the rectangle together and seal it to give it a spherical shape.
7. Brush each pizza pastries with the butter mixture, place it in the baking dish,and try not to jam-pack the baking dish And at this point you may need cook in batches.
8. Place it inside your air fryer and cook it for 15 minutes.
9. Thereafter, carefully remove the pizza pastries from your air fryer and cook any leftovers.
10.   Serve and enjoy!

Nutritional Information per serving:

Calories: 210, Fat: 9g, Protein: 7g, Dietary Fiber; 1g, Carbohydrates: 27g

16. Scrumptious Baked Sweet Potato

Time: 40 minutes

Yield: 3

Ingredients:

- 3 sweet potatoes
- 1 tablespoon of olive oil
- 1 tablespoon of freshly chopped parsley
- 2 teaspoons of salt
- 1 teaspoon of black pepper
- 3 tablespoons of butter
- Sour cream (for serving)

Instructions:

1. Preheat your air fryer to 390 degrees Fahrenheit.
2. Wash and scrub the sweet potatoes.
3. Use a fork to poke some holes in your sweet potatoes.
4. Then sprinkle the olive oil, salt and black pepper over the sweet potatoes.
5. Place the sweet potatoes inside your air fryer and cook it for 40 minutes or until it gets soft.
6. Thereafter, carefully remove the sweet potatoes from your air fryer and cut it vertically.
7. Add one tablespoon of butter in each sweet potato and top it with the sour cream and parsley.
8. Serve and enjoy!

Nutritional Information per serving:

Calories: 150, Fat: 4g, Protein: 2g, Dietary Fiber: 3g,

Carbohydrates: 25g

17. Jamaican Chicken Meatballs

Time: 20 minutes

Yield: 4

Ingredients:

- 2 boneless, skinless chicken breasts
- 1 peeled and chopped onion
- 2 tablespoons of honey
- 3 tablespoons of soy sauce
- 1 teaspoon of chili powder
- 1 tablespoon of dried thyme
- 1 tablespoon of dried basil
- 1 tablespoon of dried cumin
- 1 tablespoon of mustard powder
- 2 teaspoons of jerk paste
- 1 teaspoon of salt
- 1 teaspoon of black pepper

Instructions:

1. Preheat your air fryer to 360 degrees Fahrenheit.
2. Using a food processor, add the chicken and blend it until it is minced.
3. Add the onions and blend it until it mixes properly.
4. Add all the seasonings, herbs and blend it until it mixes properly.
5. Remove the minced chicken mixture from your blender and shape it into meatballs.
6. Grease your air fryer tray with a nonstick cooking spray and add the meatballs.
7. Cook the meatballs for 15 minutes at a 360 degrees Fahrenheit.
8. When the cooking is done, stick them onto the skewers
9. Serve and enjoy!

Nutritional Information per serving:

Calories: 190, Fat: 3g, Protein: 28g, Dietary Fiber: 3g,

Carbohydrates: 10g

18. Royal Meatball Sub

Time: 30 minutes

Yield: 3

Ingredients:

- 3 baguettes
- 1 (15-ounce) can of tomato sauce
- 4 slices of provolone cheese
- 1 pound of ground beef
- 1 peeled and chopped onion
- ¼ cup of panko breadcrumbs
- 1 egg
- ½ cup of shredded cheddar cheese
- 1 tablespoon of olive oil
- 1 tablespoon of dried oregano
- 1 tablespoon of dried parsley
- 1 teaspoon of salt
- 1 teaspoon of black pepper

Instructions:

1. Preheat your air fryer to 360 degrees Fahrenheit.
2. Using a bowl, add the ground beef, seasonings, onion, breadcrumbs, egg and stir until it is properly mixed
3. Mold the ground beef mixture into separate meatballs.

4. Then grease your air fryer, add the meatballs and cook it for 15 minutes at 360 degrees Fahrenheit or until the meatballs gets brown in color.
5. At the same time, cut the baguette into two halves, brush it with olive oil and toast the baguettes until it is lightly toasted.
6. Once the meatballs are cooked, remove and set it aside.
7. Then using a large heat-safe bowl, add the canned tomato sauce and place it inside your air fryer.
8. Cook it for at a 360 degrees Fahrenheit or until the tomato sauce has been fully heated thoroughly, and pour in the meatballs until it is covered with the sauce. (Alternatively, you can do this step in a saucepan.)
9. Add the meatballs and tomato sauce to each toasted baguette.
10. Top the meatballs with provolone cheese, place it inside your oven and allow it to melt. Then Carefully cut the baguette into separate servings.
11. Serve and enjoy!

Nutritional Information per serving:

Calories: 390, Fat: 9g, Protein: 26g, Dietary Fiber: 6g,

Carbohydrates: 50g

19. Savory Fried Eggplant

Time: 20 minutes

Yield: 2

Ingredients:

- 1 eggplant, peeled and cut into ½-inch slices
- 1 teaspoon of salt

- 1 teaspoon of black pepper
- ½ cup of flour
- 2 eggs, beaten
- 1 cup of panko breadcrumbs
- 1 pound of shredded mozzarella cheese
- 1 jar of marinara sauce

Instructions:

1. Preheat your air fryer to 390 degrees Fahrenheit.
2. Using a bowl, add the flour.
3. Then using a second bowl, beat the eggs into it.
4. Thereafter use a third bowl, and add the breadcrumbs.
5. Coat the eggplant slices in the flour, dip it into the egg wash and then cover it with the panko breadcrumbs.
6. Working in batches, add 5 eggplant slices into your air fryer and cook it for 8 minutes.
7. Thereafter, carefully remove the eggplant slices from your air fryer and season it with salt and black pepper. Repeat this with any remaining eggplant rounds.
8. Serve and enjoy!

Nutritional Information per serving:

Calories: 260, Fat: 10g, Protein: 8g, Dietary Fiber: 4g,

Carbohydrates: 35g

20. Awesome Air-Fried Ravioli

Time: 15 minutes

Yield: 6

Ingredients:

- 1 jar of marinara sauce
- 1 box of ravioli
- 1 tablespoon of olive oil
- 1 cup of buttermilk
- ½ cup of Parmesan cheese
- 2 cups of breadcrumbs

Instructions:

1. Using a bowl, add the buttermilk.
2. Then place a second bowl, add the breadcrumbs and a tiny amount of oil.
3. Dip the ravioli in the buttermilk and cover it with the breadcrumbs.
4. Place the coated ravioli in your air fryer on the baking paper and cook it for 5 minutes at a 200 degrees Fahrenheit.
5. Serve and enjoy with the marinara sauce!

Nutritional Information per serving:

Calories: 250, Fat: 4g, Protein: 10g, Carbohydrates: 43g,

Dietary Fiber: 2g

Chapter 4: Air Fryer Dinner Recipes

21. Turkey Breast with Maple Mustard Glaze

Time: 45 minutes

Yield: 6

Ingredients:

- 5-pound of a whole turkey breast
- 1 tablespoon of olive oil
- 1 teaspoon of dried thyme
- 1 teaspoon of dried oregano
- 1 teaspoon of dried parsley
- 1 teaspoon of paprika
- 1 teaspoon of salt
- 1 teaspoon of black pepper
- ¼ cup of maple syrup
- 2 tablespoons of Dijon mustard
- 1 tablespoon of melted unsalted butter

Instructions:

1. Preheat your air fryer to 360 degrees Fahrenheit.
2. Brush 1 tablespoon of olive oil over the turkey breast.
3. Using a small bowl, mix the dried thyme, dried oregano, dried parsley, paprika, salt, black pepper and then rub the turkey breast with the herb and spice mixture.
4. Place the seasoned turkey breast into your air fryer basket and cook it for 25 minutes.
5. After 25 minutes, flip the turkey breast and cook it for an additional 12 minutes or until the turkey is entirely done.
6. Using a saucepan, add the maple syrup, Dijon mustard and the butter, on an average temperature of heat.

7. Brush the turkey breast with the maple mustard, glaze it all over and place the back inside your air fryer.
8. Cook it for an additional 5 minutes or until the skin is crispy and brown.
9. Then remove it from your air fryer and allow it to cool off for a couple of minutes.
10. Serve and enjoy!

Nutritional Information per serving:

Calories: 180, Fat: 1g, Protein: 35g, Dietary fiber: 1g, Carbohydrates: 7g

22. General Wong's Beef and Broccoli
Time: 25 minutes (plus 30 minutes for marinating)

Yield: 4

Ingredients:

- 1 pound of steak, sliced into strips
- 1 pound of stemmed and chopped into florets broccoli
- 1/3 cup of oyster sauce
- 1/3 cup of sherry
- 1 tablespoon of minced ginger
- 1 tablespoon of minced garlic
- 1 tablespoon of olive oil
- 1 tablespoon of soy sauce
- 1 tablespoon of sesame oil
- 1 teaspoon of cornstarch

Instructions:

1. Using a bowl, add the oyster sauce, sherry, minced ginger, minced garlic, olive oil, soy sauce, sesame oil, cornstarch and stir it until it is properly mixed.
2. Then, add the steak, broccoli, cover it well and allow it to marinate for 30 minutes or overnight.
3. Then preheat your air fryer to 360 degrees Fahrenheit.
4. After marinating, place the marinade steak and broccoli in your air fryer.
5. Cook it for 15 minutes at a 360 degrees Fahrenheit or until it is done.
6. Serve and enjoy along with the white rice!

Nutritional Information per serving:

Calories: 340, Fat: 21g, Protein: 21g, Dietary Fiber: 2.5g, Carbohydrates: 18g

23. Irresistible Meatloaf

Time: 25 minutes

Yield: 4

Ingredients:

- 1 ½ pound of lean ground beef
- 1 beaten egg
- 1 cup of panko breadcrumbs
- 1/3 cup of steak sauce
- 1 finely chopped onion
- 1 chopped green bell pepper
- ½ cup of chopped mushrooms
- 1 tablespoon of chopped thyme
- 1 teaspoon of paprika

- 1 teaspoon of garlic powder
- 1 teaspoon of salt
- 1 teaspoon of black pepper

Instructions:

1. Preheat your air fryer to 390 degrees Fahrenheit.
2. Using a large bowl, add all the ingredients and stir until it mixes properly.
3. Thereafter, grease a heat-safe pan or the air fryer baking accessory with a nonstick cooking spray.
4. Add the mixed ground beef into the pan or baking accessory and flatten the top.
5. After that, place the pan or accessory inside your air fryer and cook it for 25 minutes at a 390 degrees Fahrenheit or until it gets brown and done.
6. Thereafter, carefully remove it from your air fryer and allow it to cool off before serving.
7. Serve and enjoy!

Nutritional Information per serving:

Calories: 300, Fat: 18g, Protein: 23g, Dietary fiber: 0.7g, Carbohydrates: 9g

24. Rockstar Rib Eye-Steak

Time: 20 minutes

Yield: 1 or 2

Ingredients:

- 2 pounds of rib-eye steak
- 1 tablespoon of olive oil

- 1 teaspoon of salt
- 1 teaspoon of black pepper
- 1 teaspoon of ground coriander
- 1 teaspoon of brown sugar
- 1 teaspoon of sweet paprika
- 1 teaspoon of mustard powder
- 1 teaspoon of onion powder
- 1 teaspoon of chili powder
- 1 teaspoon of garlic powder

Instructions:

1. Preheat your air fryer to 390 degrees Fahrenheit.
2. Sprinkle the olive oil over the rib-eye steak.
3. Season the steak on all sides with all the listed seasonings until it is well covered.
4. Place the steak into your air fryer basket.
5. Cook it for 8 minutes at a 390 degrees Fahrenheit.
6. After 8 minutes, flip the steak over and cook for an additional 7 minutes.
7. When done, carefully remove the steak from your air fryer and allow it to cool off before serving.
8. Serve and enjoy!

Nutritional Information per serving:

Calories: 520, Fat: 35g, Dietary Fiber: 0g, Carbohydrates: 2g, Protein: 56g

25. Unimaginable Zucchini Bacon Lasagna

Time: 30 minutes

Yield: 4

Ingredients:

- 2 thinly sliced zucchinis
- 6 strips of bacon
- 2 cups of grated ricotta cheese
- 2 cups of grated mozzarella cheese
- 2 teaspoons of onion powder
- 1 teaspoon of garlic powder
- 1 teaspoon of salt
- 1 teaspoon of black pepper

Instructions:

1. Preheat your air fryer to 390 degrees Fahrenheit.
2. Grease a lasagna pan with a nonstick cooking spray.
3. Using a bowl, add and mix the ricotta cheese, mozzarella cheese, onion powder, garlic powder, salt, and the black pepper properly.
4. Cut the zucchini into layers and place it in the lasagna pan.
5. Add the seasoned cheese mixture.
6. Then, add the bacon and sprinkle it with the seasoned cheese.
7. Repeat this again by layering the zucchini, cheese, bacon, until all the ingredients has been used.
8. Place the lasagna pan in your oven and cook it for 15 minutes or until the cheese gets melted.
9. Serve and enjoy!

Nutritional Information per serving:

Calories: 335, Fat: 12g, Protein: 16g, Dietary Fiber: 5g, Carbohydrates: 40g

26. Fantastic Garlic Butter Pork Chops
Time: 20 minutes

Yield: 4

Ingredients:

- 4 pork chops
- ¼ cup of melted butter
- 1 tablespoon of olive oil
- 4 minced garlic cloves
- 2 tablespoons of thinly sliced parsley
- 1 teaspoon of salt
- 1 teaspoon of black pepper

Instructions:

1. Preheat your air fryer to 360 degrees Fahrenheit.
2. Using a bowl, add and mix all the ingredients except for the pork chops properly.
3. Brush the mixture on all the dimensions of the pork sides.
4. Grease your air fryer and place it on the pork chops inside.
5. Cook it for 7 minutes at a 360 degrees Fahrenheit.
6. After 7 minutes, flip the pork chops and cook it for an additional 7 minutes.
7. Serve and enjoy!

Nutritional Information per serving:

Calories: 200, Fat: 6g, Protein: 20g, Dietary Fiber: 0.2g, Carbohydrates: 18g

27. Super-Yummy Roast Pork Belly
Time:

Yield: 2

Ingredients:

- 2 pounds of pork belly
- 2 teaspoons of garlic powder
- 2 teaspoons of onion powder
- 1 teaspoon of smoked paprika
- 1 teaspoon of salt
- 2 teaspoons of five-spice powder
- 2 teaspoons of rosemary
- 1 teaspoon of black pepper

Instructions:

1. Fill a large pot with enough water, boil it and then add the pork belly into the hot water for 10 minutes.
2. Then remove it from the boiling water and allow it to dry for 3 hours or until it dries completely.
3. Use a fork to poke some holes all around the pork belly.
4. While still doing that, using a small mixing bowl, add and mix all the seasonings together, then rub the pork belly with the seasonings.
5. Preheat your air fryer to 320 degrees Fahrenheit.
6. Place the pork belly inside your air fryer and cook it for 30 minutes.
7. Increase the temperature to 360 degrees Fahrenheit and cook it for an additional 20 minutes.
8. Serve and enjoy!

Nutritional Information per serving:

Calories: 240, Fat: 20g, Protein: 13g, Dietary Fiber: 0g, Carbohydrates: 1g

28. Outstanding Rack of Lamb

Time: 25 minutes

Yield: 4

Ingredients:

- 2 racks of lamb
- ¼ cup of freshly chopped parsley
- 4 cloves of minced garlic
- 2 tablespoons of olive oil
- 2 tablespoons of honey
- 1 teaspoon of salt
- 1 teaspoon of black pepper

Instructions:

1. Preheat your air fryer to 390 degrees Fahrenheit.
2. Using a blender or food processor, add the parsley, garlic cloves, olive oil, honey, salt, and black pepper and blend it until it gets totally grounded.
3. Rub the grounded parsley-garlic on the lamb racks, without using them all as you will need them later.
4. Put the grill pan accessory into your air fryer, and place the lamb racks on top.
5. Cook it for 15 minutes at a 390 degrees Fahrenheit or until it gets brown in color.
6. Spread another layer of the puree on the lamb racks.
7. Serve and enjoy!

Nutritional Information per serving:

Calories: 335, Fat: 26g, Protein: 21g, Dietary Fiber: 0g, Carbohydrates: 2.5g

29. Phenomenal Herbed Roast Beef

Time: 1 hour

Yield: 4

Ingredients:

- 4-pound roasted beef
- 1 tablespoon of olive oil
- 1 teaspoon of salt
- 1 teaspoon of black pepper
- 1 teaspoon of dried thyme
- 1 tablespoon of freshly chopped rosemary
- 1 tablespoon of freshly chopped parsley

Instructions:

1. Preheat your air fryer to 360 degrees Fahrenheit.
2. Using a bowl, add and mix the olive oil, salt, black pepper, thyme, rosemary, parsley properly.
3. Rub the mixture all over the roasted beef.
4. Place the beef inside your air fryer basket and cook it for 20 minutes.
5. After 20 minutes, flip the beef over and cook for an additional 30 minutes or until it reaches your desired preference.
6. Remove the roasted beef and allow it to cool of before serving.
7. Serve and enjoy!

Nutritional Information per serving:

Calories: 210, Fat: 10g, Protein: 27g, Dietary Fiber: 0.2g, Carbohydrates: 0.6g

30. Remarkable Air-Fried Ham with Honey and Brown Sugar Glaze

Time: 1 hour

Yield: 6

Ingredients:

- 4-pound of fully cooked slice ham
- 1 cup of pineapple juice
- 1 cup of brown sugar
- ½ cup of honey
- 2 orange juice
- 1 teaspoon of salt

Instructions:

1. Preheat your air fryer to 350 degrees Fahrenheit.
2. Grease your air fryer basket with a nonstick cooking spray and add the 4-pound ham or a big sized ham that can fit properly into your air fryer.
3. Cook the ham for 15 minutes at a 350 degrees Fahrenheit.
4. While still doing that, using a saucepan, add and mix 1 cup of pineapple juice, 1 cup of brown sugar, ½ cup of honey, the 2 orange juices, and 1 teaspoon of salt properly.
5. Simmer the pineapple-glaze mixture using an average temperature of heat until the glaze has thickened.
6. After the 15 minutes has elapsed, open your air fryer and pour half of the glaze on top of the ham. Cook the ham for an additional 25 minutes inside your air fryer at a 350 degrees or until it is done.
7. Once its done, carefully remove the ham from your air fryer and pour the remaining half of the sauce over.
8. Serve and enjoy!

Nutritional Information per serving:

Calories: 180, Fat: 0.7g, Dietary Fiber: 0.5g, Carbohydrates: 38g, Protein: 4g

31. Amazing Lamb Chops with Herbed Garlic Sauce

Time: 25 minutes

Yield: 4

Ingredients:

- 4 lamb chops
- 1 garlic bulb
- 1 tablespoon of freshly chopped parsley
- 1 tablespoon of freshly chopped oregano
- 2 tablespoons of olive oil
- 1 teaspoon of onion powder
- 1 teaspoon of salt
- 1 teaspoon of black pepper

Instructions:

1. Preheat your air fryer to 390 degrees Fahrenheit.
2. Brush the garlic bulb with an olive oil and place it inside your air fryer,cook it for 12 minutes or until it is properly roasted, then remove it from your air fryer and set it aside.
3. Using a small bowl, mix the parsley, oregano, olive oil, onion powder, salt, and the black pepper properly.
4. Thereafter spread each lamb chop with about one teaspoon of the herbed olive oil mixture.
5. Place the lamb chops into your air fryer and cook it for 6 minutes at a 390 degrees Fahrenheit or until it turns brown.

6. Press the garlic cloves with a garlic press and mix it properly with the herbed olive oil.
7. Spread the garlic sauce over the lamb chops.
8. Serve and enjoy!

Nutritional Information per serving:

Calories: 180, Fat: 8g, Protein: 23g, Carbohydrates: 1.7g, Dietary Fiber: 0.5g

Chapter 5: Air Fryer Appetizer Recipes

32. Spanish Spicy Potatoes

Time: 30 minutes

Yield: 4

Ingredients:

- 3 peeled and sliced into chips potatoes
- 1 peeled and chopped onion
- 1 (8-ounce) can of tomato sauce
- 1 finely chopped tomato
- 1 tablespoon of red wine vinegar
- 2 tablespoons of olive oil
- 1 teaspoon of smoked paprika
- 1 teaspoon of chili powder
- 2 teaspoons of ground coriander
- 2 teaspoons of thyme
- 1 teaspoon of dried oregano
- 1 teaspoon of dried rosemary
- 1 teaspoon of salt
- 1 teaspoon of black pepper

Instructions:

1. Cover your potatoes with a tablespoon of olive oil and place it inside your air fryer.
2. Cook it at a 360 degrees Fahrenheit for 15 minutes or until the fork gets soft.
3. While doing that, using a small bowl, mix the remaining ingredients and transfer it to a heat-safe bowl or a baking dish.

4. When the potatoes are done, remove them from your air fryer and place it in the baking dish with the tomato sauce inside.
5. Cook it for 8 minutes or until it is well heated . Alternatively, you can use a microwave or a saucepan.
6. Once done, carefully pour the tomato sauce mixture over the potatoes.
7. Serve and enjoy!

Nutritional Information per serving:

Calories: 210, Fat: 8g, Protein: 12g, Dietary Fiber: 4g, Carbohydrates: 25g

33. Astonishing Chicken Kebabs

Time: 15 minutes

Yield: 2

Ingredients:

- 2 chopped boneless, skinless chicken breasts
- 6 halves of mushrooms
- 1 chopped red bell pepper
- 1 chopped green bell pepper
- 1 chopped yellow bell pepper
- 1/3 cup of honey
- 1/3 cup of soy sauce
- 1 teaspoon of salt
- 1 teaspoon of black pepper
- Wooden skewers

Instructions:

1. Preheat your air fryer to 340 degrees Fahrenheit.

2. Using a bowl, add and mix 1/3 cup of honey, 1/3 cup of soy sauce, salt, and black pepper.
3. For each wooden skewer, add the bell peppers, chicken, and mushroom slices.
4. Thereafter, brush the chicken kabobs with the honey soy sauce mixture.
5. Place the chicken kabobs into your air fryer basket and cook it for 15 to 20 minutes.
6. Serve and enjoy!

Nutritional Information per serving:

Calories: 90, Fat: 4g, Protein: 8g, Dietary Fiber: 1g, Carbohydrates: 6g

34. Appetizing Avocado Fries
Time: 20 minutes

Yield: 4

Ingredients:

- 2 avocados, peeled, pitted, and sliced into fries
- 1 cup of panko breadcrumbs
- 1 teaspoon of salt

Instructions:

1. Preheat your air fryer to 390 degrees Fahrenheit.
2. Using a bowl, mix the panko breadcrumbs with 1 teaspoon of salt.
3. Dredge the avocado fries into the panko breadcrumb mixture until it is properly covered.
4. Place the avocado fries inside your air fryer, cook it for 10 minutes and then shake it 5 minutes after that.
5. Serve and enjoy!

Nutritional Information per serving:

Calories: 130, Fat: 11g, Protein: 4g, Dietary Fiber: 4g, Carbohydrates: 6g

35. Godly Pork Taquitos

Time: 25 minutes

Yield: 4

Ingredients:

- 30-ounces of cooked and shredded pork tenderloin
- 2 ½ cups of shredded mozzarella cheese
- 10 small whole wheat tortillas
- 1 lime juice

Instructions:

1. Preheat your air fryer to 380 degrees Fahrenheit.
2. Stir the lime juice over the shredded pork tenderloins.
3. Soften the tortillas in your air fryer by microwaving it for 10 seconds.
4. For each tortilla add 3-ounces of the shredded pork and ¼ cup of the mozzarella cheese.
5. lightly roll up the tortillas.
6. Then spray a nonstick cooking spray over the tortillas and place it inside your air fryer.
7. Cook it for 7 to 10 minutes or until it gets a golden brown color, and then flip after 5 minutes.
8. Serve and enjoy!

Nutritional Information per serving:

Calories: 210, Fat: 9g, Protein: 7g, Dietary Fiber: 3g, Carbohydrates: 25g

36. Tasteful Air-Fried Spiced Chickpeas

Time: 20 minutes

Yield: 4

Ingredients:

- 1 (15-ounce) can of drained and rinsed chickpeas
- 1 tablespoon of olive oil
- 1 teaspoon of sweet paprika
- 1 teaspoon of ground cumin
- 1 teaspoon of salt

Instructions:

1. Preheat your air fryer to 390 degrees Fahrenheit.
2. Using a bowl, add all the ingredients and toss it until it is properly mixed.
3. Working in batches, add the chickpeas inside your air fryer and cook it for 8 to 10 minutes or until it gets crispy, then after 5 minutes you can then shake it. Repeat this with the remaining batches.
4. Thereafter, carefully remove the chickpeas from your air fryer and place it into a bowl.
5. Serve and enjoy!

Nutritional Information per serving:

Calories: 70, Fat: 1g, Protein: 4g, Dietary Fiber: 3g, Carbohydrates: 11g

37. Gourmet Potato Chips

Time: 1 hour

Yield: 4

Ingredients:

- 1 pound of potatoes
- 1 tablespoon of duck fat
- 1 teaspoon of salt (to taste)

Instructions:

1. Scrub the potatoes with a hot water and peel it using a knife or potato peeler.
2. Thinly slice the potatoes into chips using a knife or a mandolin.
3. Fill a large pot with cold water, add the potato slices to it and allow it to soak for 30 minutes.
4. Drain the potato slices and pat it dry with a cloth.
5. Preheat your air fryer to 360 degrees Fahrenheit.
6. Place the potato chips into your air fryer and top it with the duck fat.
7. Cook it for 25 to 30 minutes, while shaking it at a constant interval rate of 10 minutes to prevent sticking.
8. Serve and enjoy!

Nutritional Information per serving:

Calories: 230, Fat: 10g, Protein: 3g, Dietary Fiber: 2g, Carbohydrates: 32g

38. Seasoned Tater Tots

Time: 23 minutes

Yield: 4

Ingredients:

- 1 (32-ounce) bag of frozen tater tots
- 2 tablespoons of olive oil
- 1 teaspoon of garlic powder
- 1 teaspoon of chili powder
- 1 tablespoon of Italian seasoning
- 1 teaspoon of salt
- 1 teaspoon of black pepper

Instructions:

1. Preheat your air fryer to 390 degrees Fahrenheit.
2. Using a bowl, mix and toss the tater tots, olive oil, garlic powder, chili powder, Italian seasoning, salt, and the black pepper properly.
3. Then grease your air fryer basket with a nonstick cooking spray and add the tater tots to it.
4. Thereafter cook it for 10 minutes at a 390 degrees Fahrenheit or until it has a golden brown color and a crispy texture.
5. When the cooking is done, transfer it to a bowl or a plate and allow it to cool off.
6. Serve and enjoy!

Nutritional Information per serving:

Calories: 160, Fat: 8g, Protein: 2g, Dietary Fiber: 2g, Carbohydrates: 20g

39. Gratifying Stuffed Mushrooms
Time: 35 minutes

Yield: 2

Ingredients:

- 6 mushrooms
- ½ cup of peeled and chopped onion
- 1 tablespoon of breadcrumbs
- 1 teaspoon of garlic puree
- 1 tablespoon of olive oil
- 1 teaspoon of freshly chopped parsley
- 1 teaspoon of salt
- 1 teaspoon of black pepper

Instructions:

1. Using a bowl, add the onion, breadcrumbs, garlic puree, olive oil, parsley, salt, and black pepper.
2. Remove the middle stalk of each mushroom and fill them with the onion mixture.
3. Grease your air fryer basket and place the stuffed mushrooms into it.
4. Cook it for 10 minutes at a 360 degrees Fahrenheit.
5. Once done, carefully remove it from your air fryer and cook it for 10 minutes.
6. Serve and enjoy!

Nutritional Information per serving:

Calories: 80, Fat; 4g, Protein: 6g, Carbohydrates: 5g, Dietary Fiber: 2.5g

40. Enticing Air-Fried Onion Rings
Time: 15 minutes

Yield: 2

Ingredients:

- 1 cup of oats
- 1 onion rings
- 1 beaten egg
- 1 teaspoon of salt
- 1 teaspoon of black pepper

Instructions:

1. Preheat your air fryer to 360 degrees Fahrenheit.
2. Using a bowl, add the eggs and mix properly.
3. Then using a food processor, add the oats and beat it until it appears like the breadcrumbs, thereafter transfer it to a bowl.
4. Dredge the onion rings into the oats, immerse it into the egg wash, and cover it with the oats again.
5. Grease your air fryer basket and add the onion rings.
6. Cook it for 8 minutes at a 360 degrees Fahrenheit.
7. Serve and enjoy!

Nutritional Information per serving:

Calories: 300, Fat: 18g, Protein: 4g, Dietary Fiber: 2g, Carbohydrates: 31g

41. Crispy Dumplings

Time: 18 minutes

Yield: 2

Ingredients:

- ½ pound of ground pork

- ½ packet of dumpling wrappers
- ½ teaspoon of salt
- ½ teaspoon of black pepper
- 1 tablespoon of olive oil

Instructions:

1. Preheat your air fryer to 390 degrees Fahrenheit.
2. Using a bowl, add and mix the ½ pound of ground pork, ½ teaspoon of salt, and the ½ teaspoon of black pepper properly.
3. For each dumpling wrapper add around 2 teaspoons of the ground pork mixture.
4. Seal the dumpling wrapper edges using water and try to create a triangular figure.
5. Grease your air fryer basket with a nonstick cooking spray and add the dumplings.
6. Cook the dumplings for 8 minutes or until it turns golden brown in color.
7. Serve and enjoy!

Nutritional Information per serving:

Calories: 320, Fat: 7g, Protein: 17g, Dietary Fiber: 1.6g, Carbohydrates: 45g

42. Everyday Chicken Nuggets

Time: 17 minutes

Yield: 2

Ingredients:

- 1 pound of boneless, skinless chicken breasts, cut into 1-inch pieces

- 1 beaten egg
- 1 cup of milk
- 2 cups of flour
- 1 cup of breadcrumbs
- 2 teaspoons of salt
- 1 teaspoon of black pepper
- 1 teaspoon of sweet paprika

Instructions:

1. Preheat your air fryer to 360 degrees Fahrenheit.
2. Using a bowl, mix the eggs and milk properly.
3. Pick a second bowl, add the flour and place it aside.
4. Then using a third bowl, add the breadcrumbs, salt, black pepper, sweet paprika and mix properly.
5. Dredge the chicken pieces in the flour, soak the chicken pieces into the egg wash, and then cover it with the seasoned breadcrumbs.
6. Place the chicken pieces in your air fryer and cook it for 10 minutes at a 360 degrees Fahrenheit or until it has a golden brown color, flipping halfway through.
7. Serve and enjoy!

Nutritional Information per serving:

Calories: 190, Fat: 9g, Protein: 7g, Dietary Fiber: 1g, Carbohydrates: 20g

43. Fresh Air-Fried Croutons

Time: 10 minutes

Yield: 2

Ingredients:

- 3 wholemeal bread slices
- 1 tablespoon of melted butter
- 1 tablespoon of olive oil
- ½ teaspoon of garlic powder
- ½ teaspoon of onion powder
- ½ teaspoon of dried oregano
- ½ teaspoon of dried basil

Instructions:

1. Preheat your air fryer to 390 degrees Fahrenheit.
2. Chop your bread slices into chunks.
3. Using a bowl, mix the butter, olive oil, garlic powder, onion powder, dried oregano and the dried basil.
4. Brush the bread slices with the mixture.
5. Cook for 8 minutes at a 390 degrees Fahrenheit.
6. Serve and enjoy over the salads, soups, or as a light snack.

Nutritional Information per serving:

Calories: 40, Fat: 2g, Protein: 1g, Carbohydrates: 6g, Dietary Fiber: 0.5g

44. Not Your Average Garlic Potatoes

Time: 25 minutes

Yield: 2

Ingredients:

- 6 peeled and chopped Yukon potatoes
- 4 slices of cooked and crumbled bacon

- 1 tablespoon of olive oil
- 1 teaspoon of garlic puree
- 1 teaspoon of salt
- 1 teaspoon of black pepper

Instructions:

1. Preheat your air fryer to 390 degrees Fahrenheit.
2. Sprinkle the potato chunks with olive oil.
3. Place it inside your air fryer and cook it for 10 minutes at a 390 degrees Fahrenheit.
4. Using a bowl, mix the remaining ingredients.
5. Once the potatoes is done, add the mixture to the potatoes.
6. Transfer it to a whole piece of aluminum foil and wrap it up to a smaller degree.
7. Place it back in your air fryer and cook for about 10 minutes at a 390 degrees Fahrenheit.
8. Serve and enjoy!

Nutritional Information per serving:

Calories: 130, Fat: 6g, Protein: 2g, Dietary Fiber: 1g, Carbohydrates: 18g

45. Rosemary Roasted Potatoes

Time: 15 minutes

Yield: 2

Ingredients:

- 2 peeled and chopped potatoes
- 1 tablespoon of chopped rosemary
- 1 tablespoon of olive oil

- 1 teaspoon of salt
- 1 teaspoon of black pepper

Instructions:

1. Sprinkle the potatoes with 1 tablespoon of olive oil and place it inside your air fryer.
2. Cook it for 10 minutes at a 390 degrees Fahrenheit.
3. Then while still doing that, using a small bowl, add the rosemary, salt and black pepper.
4. Once the potatoes are done, carefully transfer it to a bowl and sprinkle it with the seasoned rosemary.
5. Serve and enjoy!

Nutritional Information per serving:

Calories: 250, Fat: 6g, Protein: 4g, Dietary Fiber: 5g, Carbohydrates: 50g

46. Pleasant Sweet Potato Fries

Time: 20 minutes

Yield: 2

Ingredients:

- 2 sweet potatoes, cut into ½-inch pieces
- 2 tablespoons of olive oil
- 1 teaspoon of garlic powder
- 1 teaspoon of paprika
- 1 teaspoon of salt
- 1 teaspoon of black pepper

Instructions:

1. Preheat your air fryer to 360 degrees Fahrenheit.
2. Using a bowl, add the sweet potatoes and cover it with the olive oil.
3. Then place the sweet potatoes into your air fryer and cook it for 15 minutes at a 360 degrees Fahrenheit. Halfway through, shake the air fryer to prevent sticking.
4. When the sweet potatoes are done, carefully place them in a bowl, sprinkle it with the seasonings and cover it properly.
5. Serve and enjoy!

Nutritional Information per serving:

Calories: 150, Fat: 5g, Protein: 1g, Carbohydrates: 24g, Dietary Fiber: 3g

Chapter 6: Air Fryer Poultry Recipes

47. Flavorful Fried Chicken

Time: 30 minutes

Yield: 4

Ingredients:

- 4 small chicken thighs
- 1 cup of flour
- 1 cup of breadcrumbs
- 2 beaten eggs
- 1 teaspoon of salt
- 1 tablespoon of Cajun seasoning

Instructions:

1. Preheat your air fryer to 390 degrees Fahrenheit.
2. Using three bowls, add the flour to the first bowl, in the second bowl add the eggs and beat it properly, and in the third bowl add the breadcrumbs, salt, Cajun seasoning and mix properly.
3. Dredge the chicken thighs in the flour, immerse it into the egg mixture, and cover it with the breadcrumbs.
4. Grease your air fryer basket with a nonstick cooking spray and put in the 4 chicken thighs inside.
5. Cook it for 25 minutes until the chicken is crispy and turns golden brown.
6. Serve and enjoy!

Nutritional Information per serving:

Calories: 200, Fat: 12g, Protein: 19g, Dietary Fiber: 0g, Carbohydrates: 19g

48. Delectable Whole Roast Chicken

Time: 50 minutes

Yield: 4

Ingredients:

- 1 (4-pound) whole chicken
- 1 tablespoon of olive oil
- 1 teaspoon of salt
- 1 teaspoon of black pepper
- 1 teaspoon of paprika
- 1 teaspoon of onion powder
- 1 teaspoon of garlic powder
- 1 teaspoon of Italian seasoning
- 1 teaspoon of brown sugar
- 1 tablespoon of dried thyme
- 1 tablespoon of dried oregano
- 1 tablespoon of cayenne pepper

Instructions:

1. Preheat your air fryer to 340 degrees Fahrenheit.
2. Sprinkle the whole chicken with olive oil and rub the seasoning all over.
3. Grease your air fryer basket with a nonstick cooking spray and add the chicken to it.
4. Cook the chicken inside your air fryer for 30 minutes at a 340 degrees Fahrenheit.
5. After 30 minutes, flip the chicken and cook it for an additional 20 minutes or until it is totally done.
6. Serve and enjoy!

Nutritional Information per serving:

Calories: 155, Fat: 3.8g, Dietary Fiber: 0g, Carbohydrates: 0g, Protein: 28g

49. Divine Buffalo Wings

Time: 25 minutes (plus 4 hours of marinating time)

Yield: 4

Ingredients:

- 2 pounds of chicken wings
- 3 tablespoons of melted butter
- ¼ cup of hot sauce
- 1 teaspoon of paprika
- 1 teaspoon of cayenne pepper
- 1 teaspoon of salt
- 1 teaspoon of black pepper

Buffalo Sauce Ingredients:

- 3 tablespoons of melted butter
- ¼ cup of hot sauce

Instructions:

1. Using a separate bowl, add 3 tablespoons of melted butter, ¼ cup of hot sauce, paprika, cayenne pepper, salt, black pepper, chicken wings and allow it to marinate for 4 hours or overnight.
2. Preheat your air fryer to 390 degrees Fahrenheit.
3. Lubricate your air fryer basket with a nonstick cooking spray and add half of the chicken wings.
4. Cook the chicken wings for 14 minutes, then shake it 7 minutes after and repeat this with the other batch.

5. Using another bowl, add 3 tablespoons of melted butter and ¼ cup of hot sauce.
6. Remove the chicken wings from your air fryer and combine it with the buffalo sauce.
7. Serve and enjoy!

Nutritional Information per serving:

Calories: 240, Fat: 5.5g, Protein: 8g, Carbohydrates: 35g, Dietary Fiber: 6g

50. Flavorsome Honey Lime Chicken Wings

Time: 30 minutes

Yield: 4

Ingredients:

- 2 pounds of chicken wings
- ¼ cup of honey
- 2 tablespoons of lime juice
- 1 tablespoon of lime
- 1 pressed clove of garlic
- 1 teaspoon of salt
- 1 teaspoon of black pepper

Instructions:

1. Preheat your air fryer to 360 degrees Fahrenheit.
2. Using a bowl, mix the honey, lime juice, lime zest, garlic clove, salt, and black pepper.
3. Add the chicken wings and toss it until it is well covered with the honey-lime mixture.

4. Working in batches, add half of the chicken wings into the air fryer.
5. Cook it for 25 to 30 minutes or until it turns golden brown and crispy, while shaking it every 8 minutes.
6. Serve and enjoy!

Nutritional Information per serving:

Calories: 280, Fat: 0.5g, Dietary Fiber: 0.2g, Carbohydrates: 36g, Protein: 23g

51. Delightful Coconut Crusted Chicken Tenders

Time: 30 minutes

Yield: 4

Ingredients:

- 1 pound of chicken tender
- 3 beaten eggs
- 2 cups of sweetened shredded coconut
- 1 cup of cornstarch
- 1 teaspoon of salt
- 1 teaspoon of black pepper
- 1 teaspoon of cayenne pepper

Instructions:

1. Preheat your air fryer to 360 degrees Fahrenheit.
2. Using three bowls, add the cornstarch, salt, black pepper, and cayenne pepper into the first bowl. Then in the second bowl, add the eggs and beat it until it mixes properly.While in the third bowl, add the shredded coconut.

3. Dredge each chicken tender in the cornstarch mixture, then dip it into the egg wash, and then cover it with the shredded coconut.
4. Grease your air fryer with a non-stick cooking spray and add the chicken tenders.
5. Cook for 8 minutes at a 360 degrees Fahrenheit or until it turns golden brown.
6. Serve and enjoy!

Nutritional Information per serving:

Calories: 345, Fat: 11g, Protein: 32g, Carbohydrates: 29g, Dietary Fiber: 2.4g

52. Well-Tasted Popcorn Chicken
Time: 20 minutes

Yield: 2

Ingredients:

- 2 boneless, skinless chicken breasts
- 1 cup of breadcrumbs
- 2 beaten eggs
- 1 cup of flour
- 1 teaspoon of salt
- 1 teaspoon of black pepper
- 1 teaspoon of onion powder
- 1 teaspoon of garlic powder

Instructions:

1. Preheat your air fryer to 390 degrees Fahrenheit.
2. Using a food processor, add the chicken breasts and beat it until it minced properly.

3. Using two bowls, add the flour ,the eggs and mix it properly into the first bowl, then in the second bowl, add the breadcrumbs, seasonings and mix it properly.
4. Mold the minced chicken into small balls.
5. Cover the minced chicken in the flour, dip it into the egg wash, and then cover it with the seasoned breadcrumbs.
6. Place it inside your air fryer and cook it for 10 minutes at a 390 degrees Fahrenheit or until it is fully done.
7. Serve and enjoy!

Nutritional Information per serving:

Calories: 170, Fat: 7g, Protein: 14g, Dietary fiber: 0g, Carbohydrates: 13g

53. Easy Chicken Strips
Time: 20 minutes

Yield: 2

Ingredients:

- 2 boneless, skinless chicken breasts, sliced into strips
- ½ cup of shredded coconut
- ½ cup of oats
- 1 cup of panko breadcrumbs
- 1 cup of flour
- 2 beaten eggs
- 1 teaspoon of salt
- 1 teaspoon of black pepper
- 1 teaspoon of onion powder
- ½ teaspoon of garlic powder
- 1 teaspoon of smoked paprika

Instructions:

1. Preheat your air fryer to 360 degrees Fahrenheit.
2. Firstly, slice the chicken breasts into thin strips.
3. Using a bowl, add the oats, shredded coconut, breadcrumbs, seasonings and mix properly.
4. Pick a second bowl, add the egg and mix properly, then pick another bowl, add the flour and place it aside.
5. Dredge the strips in the flour, dip the strips into the egg wash, and cover it with the coconut breadcrumb mixture.
6. Grease your air fryer basket with a nonstick cooking spray.
7. Place the chicken breasts inside your air fryer and cook it for 8 minutes at a 360 degrees Fahrenheit.
8. Reduce the heat to 340 degrees Fahrenheit and cook it for an additional 5 minutes until it is done.
9. Serve and enjoy!

Nutritional Information per serving:

Calories: 130, Fat: 12g, Protein: 14g, Carbohydrates: 8g, Dietary Fiber: 0.9g

54. Heavenly Brown Sugar Pineapple Chicken Drumsticks

Time: 15 minutes (plus 4 hours marinating time)

Yield: 4

Ingredients:

- 4 chicken drumsticks
- 1 cup of pineapple juice
- 1/3 cup of brown sugar

- 2 tablespoons of lime juice
- 2 tablespoons of ketchup
- 2 tablespoons of red wine vinegar
- 2 tablespoons of soy sauce
- 1 tablespoon of Dijon mustard
- 1 teaspoon of salt
- 1 teaspoon of black pepper
- 1 teaspoon of ginger powder
- 1 teaspoon of garlic powder
- 1 teaspoon of onion powder

Instructions:

1. Using a large bowl, add and mix the pineapple juice, brown sugar, lime juice, ketchup, red wine vinegar, soy sauce, Dijon mustard, and the seasoning properly.
2. Add the chicken tenderloins and toss them until they are properly covered.
3. Place it inside your refrigerator and allow it to marinate for 4 hours or overnight.
4. Preheat your air fryer to 390 degrees Fahrenheit.
5. Grease your air fryer basket with a nonstick cooking spray and add the drumsticks.
6. Cook it inside your air fryer for 15 minutes or until it has a brown color.
7. When done, carefully remove it from your air fryer and allow it to cool.
8. Serve and enjoy!

Nutritional Information per serving:

Calories: 190, Fat: 1.5g, Protein: 27g, Carbohydrates: 23g, Dietary Fiber: 0.2g

55. Savory Sriracha Chicken Drumsticks

Time: 1 hour

Yield: 6

Ingredients:

- 6 drumsticks
- 1 cup of sriracha
- ½ cup of honey
- ½ cup of melted butter
- 1 tablespoon of soy sauce
- 4 cloves of minced garlic
- 1 teaspoon of salt
- 1 teaspoon of black pepper

Instructions:

1. Preheat your air fryer to 390 degrees Fahrenheit.
2. Grease your air fryer basket with a nonstick cooking spray and add the chicken drumsticks.
3. Cook it inside your air fryer for 10 minutes at a 390 degrees Fahrenheit.
4. While still doing that, using a small bowl, add and mix the remaining ingredients.
5. After 10 minutes, remove the chicken drumsticks and brush it with the sriracha sauce.
6. Lower the heat to 360 degrees Fahrenheit and cook the drumsticks for an additional 10 minutes.
7. With the remaining sauce, microwave it inside your air fryer for 30 seconds or at most 1 minute.
8. Carefully remove the chicken drumsticks from your air fryer and cover it with the sriracha sauce again.
9. Serve and enjoy!

Nutritional Information per serving:

Calories: 290, Fat: 16g, Protein: 13g, Dietary Fiber: 0g, Carbohydrates: 22g

56. Chinese-Style Honey Garlic Chicken

Time: 35 minutes (plus 4 hours of marinating time)

Yield: 4

Ingredients:

- 1 pound of chicken wings
- 1 tablespoon of olive oil
- ¼ cup of soy sauce
- 3 cloves of minced garlic
- 1/3 cup of honey
- 1 teaspoon of white vinegar
- 1 teaspoon of garlic salt
- Green onions (for garnishing purpose)
- Sesame seeds (for garnishing purpose)

Instructions:

1. Using a bowl, add and mix the olive oil, soy sauce, garlic cloves, honey, white vinegar, and the garlic salt properly.
2. Add the chicken breasts and toss it until it gets properly covered.
3. Using a Ziploc bag, add the chicken wings, honey-garlic mixture and allow it to marinate for 4 hours or overnight.
4. Preheat your air fryer to 390 degrees Fahrenheit.
5. Using your baking accessory, add the chicken wings and honey-garlic mixture.

6. Place it inside your air fryer and cook it for 8 minutes at a 390 degrees Fahrenheit.
7. After 8 minutes, stir the chicken wings inside your baking accessory and cook it for an additional 10 minutes, then increase the temperature to 400 degrees Fahrenheit.
8. Garnish it with the green onions and the sesame seeds.
9. Serve and enjoy!

Nutritional Information per serving:

Calories: 200, Fat: 1.5g, Dietary Fiber: 0.1g, Carbohydrates: 18g, Protein: 27g

57. Rich Parmesan Crusted Chicken Breasts

Time: 30 minutes

Yield: 4

Ingredients:

- 4 small boneless, skinless chicken breasts
- 1 cup of panko bread crumbs
- ½ cup of Parmesan cheese
- 3 tablespoons of freshly chopped parsley
- 1 teaspoon of salt
- 1 teaspoon of black pepper
- 3 tablespoons of melted butter
- 3 tablespoons of fresh lime juice
- 2 garlic pressed cloves

Instructions:

1. Preheat your air fryer to 360 degrees Fahrenheit.

2. Using a bowl, add and mix the panko breadcrumbs, Parmesan cheese, parsley, salt, and the black pepper properly.
3. Pick another bowl, and mix the melted butter, fresh lime juice, and garlic.
4. Soak the chicken breasts into the butter mixture and cover it with the panko breadcrumb mixture until it is properly covered.
5. Grease your air fryer basket with a nonstick cooking spray and place the chicken breasts inside.
6. Cook it for 20 to 25 minutes inside your air fryer under a 360 degrees Fahrenheit of heat or until it turns golden brown and has a crispy texture.
7. Serve and enjoy!

Nutritional Information per serving:

Calories: 290, Fat: 6g, Protein: 59g, Dietary Fiber: 0.5g, Carbohydrates: 2.6g

58. Nashville Flaming Hot Breaded Chicken

Time: 35 minutes

Yield: 4

Ingredients:

- 4 medium or small chicken thighs
- 1 cup of buttermilk
- 2 beaten eggs
- ¼ cup of hot sauce

Flour Ingredients:

- 2 cups of flour
- 1 tablespoon of baking powder

- 1 tablespoon of cayenne pepper

Seasoning Spiced Rub Ingredients:

- 2 teaspoons of salt
- 2 teaspoons of paprika
- 2 teaspoons of onion powder
- 2 teaspoons of garlic powder
- 2 teaspoons of chili powder
- 2 teaspoons of black pepper
- 2 teaspoons of dried oregano
- 2 teaspoons of dried basil
- 1 tablespoon of cayenne pepper

Hot Sauce Ingredients:

- 2 tablespoons of hot sauce
- 2 tablespoons of melted butter
- 1 tablespoon of cayenne pepper
- 1 tablespoon of brown sugar
- 1 teaspoon of smoked paprika
- ¾ cup of olive oil

Instructions:

1. Using a small bowl, add and mix all the seasoning spiced rub ingredients properly.
2. Rub the chicken thighs with the seasoning mix and reserve any leftovers.
3. For the battered chicken: using a bowl, add and mix the buttermilk, eggs, and the ¼ cup of hot sauce properly.
4. Using another bowl, add 2 cups of flour, 1 tablespoon of baking powder, 1 tablespoon of cayenne pepper, any leftover spice rub and stir until it is properly mixed.
5. Dredge each chicken thigh into the flour, dip it into the buttermilk mixture and cover it with the flour once again.

6. Preheat your air fryer to 360 degrees Fahrenheit.
7. Place the chicken thighs into your air fryer and cook it for 8 minutes or until its done.
8. Thereafter, carefully remove it from your air fryer and allow it to cool off.
9. Using a small bowl, add and mix all the hot sauce ingredients, pour over the cooked chicken thighs and toss it until it is properly covered.
10. Serve and enjoy!

Nutritional Information per serving:

Calories: 380, Fat: 8g, Protein: 55g, Dietary Fiber: 3.5g, Carbohydrates: 19g

59. Desirable Korean Fried Chicken Wings

Time: 20 minutes

Yield: 4

Ingredients:

- 1 pound of chicken wings
- ½ cup of cornstarch
- 1 teaspoon of salt
- 1 teaspoon of black pepper
- 1 tablespoon of sesame seeds (for garnishing purposes)

Korean Dressing Ingredients:

- 4 tablespoons of Korean gojuchang
- 1 tablespoon of apple cider vinegar
- 1 tablespoon of melted butter
- 2 tablespoons of honey

- 1 tablespoon of soy sauce

Instructions:

1. Preheat your air fryer to 360 degrees Fahrenheit.
2. Using a bowl, season the chicken wings with the salt and black pepper.
3. Cover the chicken wings with the cornstarch.
4. Grease your air fryer basket with a nonstick cooking spray and add the chicken wings.
5. Cook it for 25 to 30 minutes or until it gets crispy, while still shaking it at a regular intervals of 8 minutes.
6. Using a bowl, add and mix all the Korean dressing ingredients properly.
7. Thereafter, carefully remove it from your air fryer and toss it with the Korean dressing mixture.
8. Garnish it with the sesame seeds.
9. Serve and enjoy!

Nutritional Information per serving:

Calories: 260, Fat: 16g, Protein: 15g, Dietary Fiber: 0.5g, Carbohydrates: 12g

60. Awesome Crispy Baked Garlic Parmesan Chicken Wings

Time: 40 minutes

Yield: 2

Ingredients:

- 1 pound of chicken wings

- 1 tablespoon of olive oil
- 2 tablespoons of melted butter
- 4 cloves of minced garlic
- 3 tablespoons of freshly chopped parsley
- 1 teaspoon of salt
- ½ cup of grated Parmesan cheese

Instructions:

1. Using a large pot, fill it with water and place a steamer basket into it.
2. Add the chicken wings on top of the steamer basket and allow it to steam for 12 minutes. Once it is done, remove it from the steamer basket and let it get cool off and dry.
3. Preheat your air fryer to 390 degrees Fahrenheit.
4. Grease your air fryer basket with a nonstick cooking spray and add the chicken wings.
5. Cook the chicken wings for 25 to 30 minutes or until it has a golden brown color and a crispy texture, while still shaking it at a regular intervals of 8minutes.
6. Using a saucepan, mix properly the olive oil, melted butter, garlic cloves, parsley, and the salt, while heating it on an average pressure of heat for 3 minutes. Thereafter remove and place it aside.
7. Remove the chicken wings from your air fryer and place it into a large bowl, pour the garlic mixture over the chicken wings and toss until it is properly covered.
8. Sprinkle the Parmesan cheese on it.
9. Serve and enjoy!

Nutritional Information per serving:

Calories: 510, Fat: 40g, Protein: 35g, Dietary Fiber: 0g, Carbohydrates: 3g

61. Spicy Teriyaki Chicken Wings

Time: 30 minutes (plus 4 hours of marinating time)

Yield: 4

Ingredients:

- 1 ½ pound of chicken wings
- ½ cup of soy sauce
- ¼ cup of rice wine vinegar
- ¼ cup of brown sugar
- 3 cloves of minced garlic
- 1 teaspoon of ginger powder
- 1 teaspoon of red pepper flakes
- 1 teaspoon of salt
- 1 teaspoon of black pepper

Instructions:

1. Using a bowl, add and mix the soy sauce, rice wine vinegar, brown sugar, garlic cloves, ginger powder, red pepper flakes, salt, and black pepper.
2. Then using a Ziploc bag, add the chicken wings, teriyaki mixture and allow it to marinate for 4 hours or overnight.
3. Preheat your air fryer to 390 degrees Fahrenheit.
4. Using your baking accessory, add the chicken wings and marinade it.
5. Place it inside your air fryer and cook it for 8 minutes at a pressure of 390 degrees Fahrenheit.
6. After 8 minutes, flip the chicken over and cook it for an additional 10 minutes, at this point increasing the temperature to 400 degrees Fahrenheit.
7. Serve and enjoy!

Nutritional Information per serving:

Calories: 220, Fat: 15g, Protein: 17g, Dietary Fiber: 0g, Carbohydrates: 3g

Chapter 7: Air Fryer Fish and Seafood

62. Remarkable Fish and Chips with Sauce

Time: 35 minutes

Yield: 4

Fish Ingredients:

- 4 cod fish fillets
- 1 teaspoon of olive oil
- 1 cup of flour
- 1 cup of panko breadcrumbs
- 2 beaten eggs

Fries Ingredients:

- 2 potatoes, cut into ½-inch strips
- 1 tablespoon of olive oil
- 1 teaspoon of salt

Sauce Ingredients:

- ¼ cup of mayonnaise
- 1 tablespoon of freshly chopped dill
- 1 tablespoon of freshly chopped tarragon
- 2 tablespoons of sour cream
- 2 tablespoons of finely chopped dill pickle
- 2 tablespoons of finely chopped red onion

Instructions:

1. Soak the potato pieces in a bowl of water for 30 minutes. After 30 minutes, drain it into a colander and pat it dry using a cloth.
2. Preheat your air fryer to 360 degrees Fahrenheit.

3. Using a large bowl, add and mix the potato strips, olive oil, salt and toss it until it is properly covered.
4. Place the potato strips inside your air fryer and cook it for 20 to 25 minutes, while still shaking it at a regular interval of 6 minutes until the potatoes reaches its golden brown color and crispy texture state. After that, remove and set it aside.
5. Then for the fish: Using a bowl, add the flour, pick another bowl, add the eggs and stir properly, then using another separate bowl, add the breadcrumbs and olive oil.
6. Dredge the cod fillets in the flour, dip it in the egg mixture, and then cover it with the breadcrumbs.
7. Grease your air fryer basket with a nonstick cooking spray and add the battered cod fillets.
8. Cook it for 10 minutes or until it has a golden brown color, carefully remove it from your air fryer basket and allow it to cool off.
9. For the sauce: Using a bowl, add all the mayonnaise, dill, tarragon, sour cream, dill pickle, the red onion, and stir it until it is properly mixed .
10.   Serve and enjoy!

Nutritional Information per serving:

Calories: 250, Fat: 8g, Protein: 13g, Dietary Fiber: 2g, Carbohydrates: 30g

63. Incredible Cajun Salmon

Time: 10 minutes

Yield: 1

Ingredients:

- 1 salmon fillet
- ½ teaspoon of salt
- ½ teaspoon of black pepper
- ½ teaspoon of garlic powder
- ½ teaspoon of onion powder
- 1 teaspoon of dried oregano
- 1 teaspoon of dried thyme
- 2 teaspoons of cayenne pepper
- 1 teaspoon of panko breadcrumbs
- 1 lime (for serving)

Instructions:

1. Preheat your air fryer to 360 degrees Fahrenheit.
2. Using a small bowl, add and mix all the seasonings, herbs, breadcrumbs and stir until it is properly mixed.
3. Cover the salmon fillet with the seasoned mixture.
4. Add the grill pan accessory in your air fryer and grease it with a nonstick cooking spray.
5. Add the salmon fillet inside and cook it for 6 minutes at a 360 degrees Fahrenheit.
6. Once done, carefully remove it from your air fryer and squeeze a lime over it.
7. Serve and enjoy!

Nutritional Information per serving:

Calories: 380, Fat: 8g, Protein: 25g, Carbohydrates: 40g, Dietary Fiber: 3.5g

64. Grand Air-Fried Coconut Shrimp

Time:

Yield: 4

Ingredients:

- 1 pound of peeled and deveined shrimp
- 1 cup of shredded coconut
- 1 cup of panko breadcrumbs
- 2 eggs
- 1/3 cup of flour
- 1 teaspoon of salt
- 1 teaspoon of black pepper

Instructions:

1. Preheat your air fryer to 360 degrees Fahrenheit.
2. Using a bowl, add and mix the flour, salt, and black pepper. Then using a second bowl, add the eggs and beat it properly. Pick a third bowl, add and mix the shredded coconut and breadcrumbs.
3. Dredge each shrimp in the flour, dip it into the egg wash and then cover it with the coconut breadcrumb mixture.
4. Grease your air fryer basket with a nonstick cooking spray and add the shrimp.
5. Cook it for 10 to 15 minutes at a 360 degrees Fahrenheit or until it has a golden brown color.
6. Serve and enjoy!

'Nutritional Information per serving:

Calories: 250, Fat: 14g, Protein: 9g, Dietary Fiber: 1.6g, Carbohydrates: 24g

65. Splendid Salmon Patties

Time: 15 minutes

Yield: 2

Ingredients:

- 1 (14-ounce) can of drained canned salmon
- ¼ cup of chopped onion
- ¼ cup of ground oats
- ¼ cup of wheat flour
- 1 egg
- ¼ cup of mayonnaise
- 1 tablespoon of parsley
- 1 teaspoon of salt
- 1 teaspoon of black pepper
- 1 cup of breadcrumbs

Instructions:

1. Preheat your air fryer to 390 degrees Fahrenheit.
2. Using a bowl, add and mix the canned salmon, onion, ground oats, wheat flour, egg, parsley, salt, black pepper and the mayonnaise properly.
3. Divide the salmon mixture into 4 patties and cover it with the breadcrumbs.
4. Add the salmon patties inside your air fryer and cook it for 8 to 10 minutes or until it has a golden brown color.
5. Serve and enjoy!

Nutritional Information per serving:

Calories: 260, Fat: 15g, Protein: 16g, Dietary Fiber: 1g, Carbohydrates: 14g

66. Breathtaking Gingered Honey Salmon

Time: 15 minutes

Yield: 1

Ingredients:

- 1 salmon fillet
- 1 teaspoon of garlic powder
- 1 teaspoon of ground ginger
- ¼ cup of honey
- 1/3 cup of soy sauce
- 1/3 cup of orange juice

Instructions:

1. Preheat your air fryer to 360 degrees Fahrenheit.
2. Using a bowl, add and mix the garlic powder, ground ginger, honey, soy sauce, and the orange juice properly.
3. Add the salmon fillet and marinate it for 30 minutes or overnight and reserve the end product.
4. Grease your air fryer basket with a nonstick cooking spray and add the salmon fillet.
5. Cook it for 5 minutes at a 360 degrees Fahrenheit.
6. Thereafter, carefully remove the fish fillet, brush the leftover marinade over and place back inside your air fryer.
7. Bring up the heat to 380 degrees Fahrenheit and cook it for an additional 5 minutes.
8. Serve and enjoy!

Nutritional Information per serving:

Calories: 265, Fat: 9g, Protein: 29g, Dietary Fiber: 0.3g, Carbohydrates: 15g

67. Japanese-Style Fried Prawns

Time: 15 minutes

Yield: 2

Ingredients:

- 1 pound of peeled and deveined prawns
- 1 cup of rice flour
- 1 cup of panko bread crumbs
- 2 eggs
- 1 teaspoon of ground ginger
- 1 tablespoon of paprika
- 1 teaspoon of salt
- 1 teaspoon of black pepper
- 1 teaspoon of garlic powder

Instructions:

1. Preheat your air fryer to 380 degrees Fahrenheit.
2. Using a bowl, add the prawns, salt, black pepper, garlic powder, ground ginger and toss until it is properly mixed.
3. Then using another bowl, add the rice flour, paprika and mix it well. Pick a second bowl, add the eggs and beat it properly. Then using a third bowl, add the panko breadcrumbs.
4. Dredge the seasoned prawns into the flour, dip it into the egg wash, and then cover it with the panko breadcrumbs.
5. Grease your air fryer basket with a nonstick cooking spray and add the prawns.
6. Cook it for 8 minutes or until it has a golden brown color and repeat if necessary.
7. Serve and enjoy!

Nutritional Information per serving:

Calories: 210, Fat: 4g, Protein: 40g, Dietary Fiber: 0g, Carbohydrates: 4g

68. Impressive Air-Fried Anchovies

Time: 8 minutes

Yield: 2

Ingredients:

- 1 pound of headless, spineless and gutless anchovies
- 1 cup of flour
- 1 teaspoon of garlic powder
- 1 teaspoon of onion powder
- 1 teaspoon of paprika
- 1 teaspoon of cumin
- 1 teaspoon of creole seasoning
- 1 teaspoon of salt
- 1 teaspoon of black pepper

Instructions:

1. Preheat your air fryer to 360 degrees Fahrenheit.
2. Using a bowl, add the flour, seasonings and mix it properly.
3. Dredge the anchovies in the seasoned flour until it is well covered.
4. Grease your air fryer basket with a nonstick cooking spray and add the coated anchovies.
5. Cook it inside your air fryer for 8 minutes or until it turns brown.
6. Serve and enjoy!

Nutritional Information per serving:

Calories: 250, Fat: 10g, Protein: 28g, Dietary Fiber: 1g, Carbohydrates: 23g

69. Great Air-Fried Soft-Shell Crab

Time:

Yield: 2

Ingredients:

- 2 soft-shell crabs
- 1 cup of flour
- 2 beaten eggs
- 1 cup of panko breadcrumbs
- 1 teaspoon of onion powder
- 1 teaspoon of garlic powder
- 1 teaspoon of salt
- 1 teaspoon of black pepper

Instructions:

1. Preheat your air fryer to 360 degrees Fahrenheit.
2. Using a bowl, add the flour, pick a second bowl, add the eggs and mix properly. Then using a third bowl, mix the panko breadcrumbs and the seasonings properly.
3. Grease your air fryer basket with a nonstick cooking spray and add the crabs inside.
4. Cook it inside your air fryer for 8 minutes or until it has a golden brown color.
5. Thereafter, carefully remove it from your air fryer and allow it to cool off.
6. Serve and enjoy!

Nutritional Information per serving:

Calories: 380, Fat: 16g, Protein: 24g, Carbohydrates: 39g, Dietary Fiber: 5g

70. Stunning Air-Fried Clams

Time: 15 minutes

Yield: 2

Ingredients:

- 1 (10-ounce) can of whole baby clams, drained and shucked
- 2 beaten eggs
- 1 cup of flour
- 1 cup of panko breadcrumbs
- 1 teaspoon of salt
- 1 teaspoon of black pepper
- 1 teaspoon of garlic powder
- 1 teaspoon of onion powder
- 1 teaspoon of cayenne pepper
- 1 tablespoon of dried oregano

Instructions:

1. Preheat your air fryer to 390 degrees Fahrenheit.
2. Using a bowl, add the flour, pick a second bowl, add the eggs and mix properly. Then using a third bowl, add and mix the panko breadcrumbs, seasonings, and the herbs properly.
3. Dredge the clams in the flour, immerse it into the egg wash and then cover it with the breadcrumb mixture.
4. Place the clams inside your air fryer and cook it for 2 minutes or until it has a golden brown color, while being cautious of overcooking.
5. Thereafter, carefully remove it from your air fryer and allow it to cool.
6. Serve and enjoy!

Nutritional Information per serving:

Calories: 225, Fat: 12g, Protein: 15g, Carbohydrates: 13g, Dietary Fiber: 0.5g

71. Mind-Blowing Air-Fried Crawfish with Cajun Dipping Sauce

Time: 10 minutes

Yield: 4

Ingredients:

- 1 pound of cooked craw-fish tail meat
- 1 beaten egg
- 4 chopped green onions
- 1 teaspoon of melted butter
- 1 teaspoon of salt
- 1 teaspoon of cayenne pepper
- 1 teaspoon of black pepper
- 1/3 cup of panko breadcrumbs
- 1/3 cup of bread flour

Sauce Ingredients:

- ¾ cup of mayonnaise
- ½ cup of ketchup
- 1 teaspoon of horseradish

Instructions:

1. Preheat your air fryer to 380 degrees Fahrenheit.
2. Using a bowl, add the eggs, green onion, butter, salt, cayenne pepper, black pepper and salt.

3. Add the panko breadcrumbs, bread flour and pour in the craw-fish, stirring it until it is properly covered.
4. Grease your air fryer basket with a nonstick cooking spray.
5. Add the battered craw-fish inside your air fryer and cook it for 5 minutes or until it has a golden brown color.
6. Thereafter, using a bowl, add the mayonnaise, ketchup, horseradish and mix properly.
7. Serve and enjoy!

Nutritional Information per serving:

Calories: 205, Fat: 6.7g, Protein: 26g, Dietary Fiber: 0.3g, Carbohydrates: 8.8g

72. Southern-Air-Fried Cat Fish

Time: 15 minutes

Yield: 4

Ingredients:

- 4 skinless catfish fillets
- 1 teaspoon of salt
- 1 teaspoon of black pepper
- 1 cup of cornmeal
- 1 cup of flour

Instructions:

1. Preheat your air fryer to 360 degrees Fahrenheit.
2. Using a bowl, add the cornmeal, flour, salt, black pepper and mix it properly.
3. Dredge the catfish fillets in the seasoned cornmeal mixture.

4. Grease your air fryer with a non-stick cooking spray and add the catfish fillets.
5. Cook the catfish for 8 minutes at a 360 degrees Fahrenheit or until it turns brown.
6. Serve and enjoy!

Nutritional Information per serving:

Calories: 350, Fat: 15g, Protein: 25g, Dietary Fiber: 0g, Carbohydrates: 36g

73. Wondrous Creole Fried Shrimp with Sriracha Sauce

Time: 10 minutes

Yield: 4

Ingredients:

- 1 pound of peeled and deveined shrimp
- ½ cup of cornmeal
- ½ cup of breadcrumbs
- 1 beaten egg
- 1 tablespoon of hot sauce
- 1 tablespoon of mustard
- 2 tablespoons of creole seasoning
- 1 teaspoon of onion powder
- 1 teaspoon of garlic powder
- 1 teaspoon of black pepper
- 1 teaspoon of salt

Siracha Sauce Ingredients:

- 1 cup of mayonnaise
- 3 tablespoons of sriracha sauce
- 1 tablespoon of soy sauce
- 1 teaspoon of black pepper

Instructions:

1. Preheat your air fryer to 360 degrees Fahrenheit.
2. Using a bowl, add the eggs, hot sauce, mustard, 1 tablespoon of creole seasoning, onion powder, garlic powder, black pepper, salt, the shrimp and toss until it is properly covered.
3. Using another bowl, add the breadcrumbs, flour, 1 tablespoon of creole seasoning, the shrimp and cover it properly.
4. Grease your air fryer basket with a nonstick cooking spray and add the shrimp.
5. Cook for it for 5 minutes or until it has a golden brown color, while being careful not to overcook.
6. Thereafter, carefully remove it from your air fryer and allow it to cool.
7. Pick a separate bowl, add and mix all the sauce ingredients properly.
8. Serve!

Nutritional Information per serving:

Calories: 200, Fat: 12g, Protein: 15g, Carbohydrates: 7g, Dietary Fiber: 0.6g

Chapter 8: Air Fryer Meat Recipes

74. Sweet and Spicy Montreal Steak

Time: 15 minutes

Yield: 2

Ingredients:

- 2 boneless sirloin steaks
- 1 tablespoon of olive oil
- 1 tablespoon of brown sugar
- 1 tablespoon of Montreal steak seasoning
- 1 teaspoon of crushed red pepper

Instructions:

1. Preheat your air fryer to 390 degrees Fahrenheit.
2. Sprinkle the sirloin steaks with olive oil.
3. Rub each steak with the brown sugar, Montreal steak seasoning, and the crushed red pepper.
4. Place the baking accessory inside your air fryer and add it to the steaks inside.
5. Cook it for 3 minutes at a 390 degrees Fahrenheit.
6. After 3 minutes has elapsed, flip the steak over and cook it for an additional 3 minutes or until it reaches your desired texture.
7. Carefully remove it from your air fryer and allow it to cool before slicing them into strips.
8. Serve and enjoy!

Nutritional Information per serving:

Calories: 160, Fat: 5g, Protein: 25g, Dietary Fiber: 0g, Carbohydrates: 3g

75. Stunning Chicken Sandwich

Time: 25 minutes

Yield: 2

Ingredients:

- 2 boneless, skinless chicken breasts
- 1 cup of flour
- 2 beaten eggs
- 1 teaspoon of garlic powder
- 1 teaspoon of onion powder
- 1 teaspoon of salt
- 1 teaspoon of black pepper
- 4 toasted hamburger buns

Instructions:

1. Using a bowl, add and mix the flour and seasonings properly. Then in a second bowl, add the eggs and beat it well.
2. Dip the chicken breasts into the egg mixture and remove any excess batter.
3. Dredge the chicken breasts in the flour mixture until it is properly coated.
4. Preheat your air fryer to 340 degrees Fahrenheit.
5. Grease your air fryer basket with a nonstick cooking spray.
6. Add the chicken breasts and cook for 6 minutes at a 340 degrees Fahrenheit.
7. Flip the chicken breasts and cook it for an additional 6 minutes.
8. Then increase the temperature to 400 degrees Fahrenheit and cook it for 2 minutes per side.
9. Serve and enjoy on the toasted hamburger buns, or with any toppings you desire!

Nutritional Information per serving:

Calories: 265, Fat: 7g, Protein: 21g, Dietary Fiber: 1.2g, Carbohydrates: 25g

76. Hearty Hot Dogs

Time: 10 minutes

Yield: 2

Ingredients:

- 2 hot dogs
- 2 hot dog buns
- Any hot dog toppings if desired

Instructions:

1. Preheat your air fryer to 390 degrees Fahrenheit.
2. Put the hot dogs inside your air fryer and cook it for 5 minutes.
3. Carefully remove it from your air fryer and allow it to cool off.
4. Place the cooked hot dogs in the bun and add any desired toppings.
5. Serve and enjoy!

Nutritional Information per serving:

Calories: 110, Fat: 10g, Protein: 5g, Dietary Fiber: 0g, Carbohydrates: 2g

77. Sweet and Sour Pork

Time: 30 minutes

Yield: 4

Ingredients:

- 2 pounds of chopped into 1-inch pieces boneless pork
- 2 beaten eggs
- 1 cup of cornstarch
- 3 tablespoons of oil
- 1 teaspoon of salt
- 1 teaspoon of black pepper

Sweet and Sour Sauce Ingredients:

- ½ cup of sugar
- 5 tablespoons of ketchup
- ½ cup of seasoned rice vinegar
- 1 tablespoon of soy sauce
- ½ teaspoon of salt

Instructions:

1. Preheat your air fryer to 340 degrees Fahrenheit.
2. Using a bowl, add the eggs and beat it properly. Pick another bowl, add and mix the cornstarch, salt, black pepper and properly and set it aside.
3. Dredge each pork chunks into the cornstarch mixture, dip it in the egg wash, and then cover it with the cornstarch mixture.
4. Grease your air fryer basket with a nonstick cooking spray.
5. Place the pork chunks in your air fryer basket and cook it for 8 to 12 minutes at a 340 degrees Fahrenheit, shaking it halfway through.
6. Then, using a saucepan, add all the sweet and sour sauce ingredients and heat it under an average pressure of heat for around 5 minutes, while still stirring consistently.
7. Once the pork turns golden brown and crispy, carefully remove it from your air fryer and allow it to cool off.
8. Serve and enjoy with the sauce!

Nutritional Information per serving:

Calories: 360, Fat: 19g, Protein: 14g, Dietary Fiber: 0g, Carbohydrates: 36g

78. Yummy Rodeo Sirloin Steaks with Coffee Rub

Time: 25 minutes

Yield: 2

Ingredients:

- 2 boneless sirloin steaks
- 1 tablespoon of olive oil
- 2 tablespoons of ground coffee
- 1 tablespoon of salt
- 1 tablespoon of brown sugar
- 1 tablespoon of dried thyme
- 1 teaspoon of garlic powder
- 1 teaspoon of black pepper

Instructions:

1. Preheat your air fryer to 390 degrees Fahrenheit.
2. Sprinkle the sirloin steak with the olive oil.
3. Using a bowl, add the ground coffee, salt, brown sugar, dried thyme, garlic powder, black pepper and mix properly.
4. Rub each sirloin steak with the coffee rub until it is properly covered.
5. Place the baking accessory inside your air fryer and add it to the steak inside.
6. Cook it for 3 minutes at a 390 degrees Fahrenheit.

7. After 3 minutes, flip the steak over and cook for an additional 3 minutes or until it reaches your desired texture.
8. Carefully remove it from your air fryer and allow it to cool before slicing.
9. Serve and enjoy!

Nutritional Information per serving:

Calories: 480, Fat: 29g, Protein: 45g, Carbohydrates: 8g, Dietary Fiber: 0.2g

Chapter 9: Air Fryer Vegetable and Sides Recipes

79. South Asian Cauliflower Fritters

Time: 25 minutes

Yield: 1

Ingredients:

- 1 large chopped into florets cauliflower
- 3 tablespoons of Greek yogurt
- 3 tablespoons of flour
- ½ teaspoon of ground turmeric
- ½ teaspoon of ground cumin
- ½ teaspoon of ground paprika
- 12 teaspoon of ground coriander
- ½ teaspoon of salt
- ½ teaspoon of black pepper

Instructions:

1. Using a large bowl, add and mix the Greek yogurt, flour, and seasonings properly.
2. Add the cauliflower florets and toss it until it is well covered
3. Preheat your air fryer to 390 degrees Fahrenheit.
4. Grease your air fryer basket with a nonstick cooking spray and add half of the cauliflower florets to it.
5. Cook it for 10 minutes or until it turns golden brown and crispy, then shake it after 5 minutes. (Repeat this with the other half).
6. Serve and enjoy!

Nutritional Information per serving:

Calories: 120, Fat: 4g, Protein: 7.5g, Carbohydrates: 14g, Dietary Fiber: 3.4g

80. Supreme Air-Fried Tofu

Time: 55 minutes

Yield: 4

Ingredients:

- 1 block of pressed and sliced into 1-inch cubes of extra-firm tofu
- 2 tablespoons of soy sauce
- 1 teaspoon of seasoned rice vinegar
- 2 teaspoons of toasted sesame oil
- 1 tablespoon of cornstarch

Instructions:

1. Using a bowl, add and toss the tofu, soy sauce, seasoned rice vinegar, sesame oil until it is properly covered.
2. Place it inside your refrigerator and allow to marinate for 30 minutes.
3. Preheat your air fryer to 370 degrees Fahrenheit.
4. Add the cornstarch to the tofu mixture and toss it until it is properly covered.
5. Grease your air fryer basket with a nonstick cooking spray and add the tofu inside your basket.
6. Cook it for 20 minutes at a 370 degrees Fahrenheit, and shake it after 10 minutes.
7. Serve and enjoy!

Nutritional Information per serving:

Calories: 80, Fat: 5.8g, Protein: 5g, Carbohydrates: 3g, Dietary Fiber: 1.2g

81. Unbelievable Roasted Winter Vegetables
Time: 20 minutes

Yield: 4

Ingredients:

- 1 pound of peeled and chopped parsnips
- 1 pound of peeled and chopped celeriac
- 1 pound of peeled and chopped butternut squash
- 1 tablespoon of freshly chopped thyme
- 2 tablespoons of olive oil
- 2 chopped red onions
- 1 teaspoon of salt
- 1 teaspoon of black pepper

Instructions:

1. Preheat your air fryer to 390 degrees Fahrenheit.
2. Using a bowl, add the parsnips, celeriac, butternut squash, and the red onions.
3. Add the olive oil, thyme, salt, black pepper and toss it until it is properly covered.
4. Put the vegetables in your air fryer basket and cook it for 20 minutes at a 390 degrees Fahrenheit or until it turns brown and soft, while still shaking it at a regular interval of 2 minutes.
5. Serve and enjoy!

Nutritional Information per serving:

Calories: 145, Fat: 4g, Protein: 2.9g, Dietary Fiber: 4g, Carbohydrates: 28g

82. Not Your Average Zucchini Parmesan Chips

Time: 15 minutes

Yield: 4

Ingredients:

- 2 thinly sliced zucchinis
- 1 beaten egg
- ½ cup of panko breadcrumbs
- ½ cup of grated Parmesan cheese
- 1 teaspoon of salt
- 1 teaspoon of black pepper

Instructions:

1. Prepare your zucchini by using a mandolin or a knife to slice the zucchinis thinly.
2. Use a cloth to pat dry the zucchini chips.
3. Then using a bowl, add the eggs and beat it properly. After that, pick another bowl, and add the breadcrumbs, Parmesan cheese, salt, and black pepper.
4. Dredge the zucchini chips into the egg mixture and then cover it with the Parmesan-breadcrumb mixture.
5. Grease the battered zucchini chips with a nonstick cooking spray and place it inside your air fryer.
6. Cook it for 8 minutes at a 350 degrees Fahrenheit.
7. Once done, carefully remove it from your air fryer and sprinkle another teaspoon of salt to give it some taste.
8. Serve and enjoy!

Nutritional Information per serving:

Calories: 100, Fat: 6g, Protein: 4g, Carbohydrates 9g, Dietary Fiber:
1.8g

83. Sky-High Roasted Corn

Time: 10 minutes

Yield: 4

Ingredients:

- 4 ears of husk-less corn
- 1 tablespoon of olive oil
- 1 teaspoon of salt
- 1 teaspoon of black pepper

Instructions:

1. Preheat your air fryer to 400 degrees Fahrenheit.
2. Sprinkle the ears of corn with the olive oil, salt and black pepper.
3. Place it inside your air fryer and cook it for 10 minutes at 400
   degrees Fahrenheit.
4. Serve and enjoy!

Nutritional Information per serving:

Calories: 100,

Fat: 1g,

Protein: 3g,

Dietary Fiber: 3g,

Carbohydrates: 22g

84. Ravishing Air-Fried Carrots with Honey Glaze

Time: 15 minutes

Yield: 2

Ingredients:

- 3 cups of chopped into ½-inch pieces carrots
- 1 tablespoon of olive oil
- 2 tablespoons of honey
- 1 tablespoon of brown sugar
- 1 teaspoon of salt
- 1 teaspoon of black pepper

Instructions:

1. Preheat your air fryer to 390 degrees Fahrenheit.
2. Using a bowl, add and toss the carrot pieces, olive oil, honey, brown sugar, salt, and the black pepper until it is properly covered.
3. Place it inside your air fryer and add the seasoned glazed carrots.
4. Cook it for 12 minutes at a 390 degrees Fahrenheit, and then shake after 6 minutes.
5. Serve and enjoy!

Nutritional Information per serving:

Calories: 90, Fat: 3.5g, Dietary Fiber: 2g, Carbohydrates: 13g, Protein: 1g

85. Flaming Buffalo Cauliflower Bites

Time: 23 minutes

Yield: 4

Ingredients:

- 1 large chopped into florets cauliflower head
- 3 beaten eggs
- 2/3 cup of cornstarch
- 2 tablespoons of melted butter
- ¼ cup of hot sauce

Instructions:

1. Preheat your air fryer to 360 degrees Fahrenheit.
2. Using a large mixing bowl, add and mix the eggs and the cornstarch a properly.
3. Add the cauliflower, gently toss it until it is properly covered with the batter, shake it off in case of any excess batter and set it aside.
4. Grease your air fryer basket with a nonstick cooking spray and add the cauliflower bites which will require you to work in batches.
5. Cook the cauliflower bites for 15 to 20 minutes or until it has a golden brown color and a crispy texture, while still shaking occasionally.
6. Then, using a small mixing bowl, add and mix the melted butter and hot sauce properly.
7. Once the cauliflower bites are done, remove it from your air fryer and place it into a large bowl. Pour the buffalo sauce over the cauliflower bites and toss it until it is properly covered.
8. Serve and enjoy!

Nutritional Information per serving:

Calories: 240, Fat: 5.5g, Dietary Fiber: 6.3g, Protein: 8.8g, Carbohydrates: 37g

86. Pleasant Air-Fried Eggplant

Time: 25 minutes

Yield: 4

Ingredients:

- 2 thinly sliced or chopped into chunks eggplants
- 1 teaspoon of salt
- 1 teaspoon of black pepper
- 1 cup of rice flour
- 1 cup of white wine

Instructions:

1. Using a bowl, add the rice flour, white wine and mix properly until it gets smooth.
2. Add the salt, black pepper and stir again.
3. Dredge the eggplant slices or chunks into the batter and remove any excess batter.
4. Preheat your air fryer to 390 degrees Fahrenheit.
5. Grease your air fryer basket with a nonstick cooking spray.
6. Add the eggplant slices or chunks into your air fryer and cook it for 15 to 20 minutes or until it has a golden brown and crispy texture, while still shaking it occasionally.
7. Carefully remove it from your air fryer and allow it to cool off.
8. Serve and enjoy!

Nutritional Information per serving:

Calories: 380, Fat: 15g, Protein: 13g, Dietary Fiber: 6.1g, Carbohydrates: 51g

87. Enriching Air-Fried Okra

Time: 25 minutes

Yield: 4

Ingredients:

- 1 pound of trimmed and sliced ½-inch thick pieces okra
- ½ cup of cornmeal
- 1 cup of flour
- ½ cup of buttermilk
- 1 teaspoon of cayenne pepper
- 1 teaspoon of onion powder
- 1 teaspoon of garlic powder
- 1 teaspoon of salt
- 1 teaspoon of black pepper

Instructions:

1. Preheat your air fryer to 350 degrees Fahrenheit.
2. Using a bowl, add and mix the flour, cornmeal, cayenne pepper, onion powder, garlic powder, salt, and black pepper properly.
3. Then pick a second bowl, and add the buttermilk.
4. Dredge each okra piece into the flour mixture, dip it into the buttermilk, dredge it into the flour mixture again and remove any excess batter.
5. Grease your air fryer basket with a nonstick cooking spray.
6. Add the okra to your air fryer basket, cook it for 10 to 15 minutes or until it has golden brown color and crispy texture at a 350 degrees Fahrenheit, which at this point may then require you to work in batches.
7. Once it is done, remove it from your air fryer and check if it's properly done. Allow it to cool off before serving.
8. Serve and enjoy!

Nutritional Information per serving:

Calories: 300, Fat: 16g, Protein: 8g, Dietary Fiber: 0g, Carbohydrates: 34g

88. Outstanding Batter-Fried Scallions

Time: 10 minutes

Yield: 4

Ingredients:

- 4 bunches of trimmed scallions
- 1 cup of flour
- 1 cup of white wine
- 1 teaspoon of salt
- 1 teaspoon of black pepper

Instructions:

1. Preheat your air fryer to 390 degrees Fahrenheit.
2. Using a bowl, add and mix the white wine, the flour and stir until it gets smooth.
3. Add the salt, the black pepper and mix again.
4. Dip each scallion into the flour mixture until it is properly covered and remove any excess batter.
5. Grease your air fryer basket with a nonstick cooking spray and add the scallions. At this point, you may need to work in batches.
6. Cook the scallions for 3 to 5 minutes or until it has a golden brown color and crispy texture, while still shaking it after every 2 minutes.
7. Carefully remove it from your air fryer and check if it's properly done. Then allow it to cool before serving.

8. Serve and enjoy!

Nutritional Information per serving:

Calories: 190, Fat: 12g, Protein: 4g, Carbohydrates: 19g, Dietary Fiber: 0.8g

89. Marvelous Parmesan Dill Fried Pickle Chips

Time: 30 minutes

Yield: 4

Ingredients:

- 1 (32-ounce) jar of large dill pickles
- 2 beaten eggs
- 1 cup of panko breadcrumbs
- 1 cup of grated Parmesan cheese
- 1 teaspoon of garlic powder
- 1 teaspoon of onion powder
- 1 teaspoon of salt
- 1 teaspoon of black pepper

Instructions:

1. Preheat your air fryer to 400 degrees Fahrenheit.
2. Using a bowl, add the eggs and beat it properly. Pick a second bowl, add the panko breadcrumbs, Parmesan cheese, seasonings and mix it properly.
3. Dip each pickle slice into the egg mixture and then cover it with the breadcrumb-cheese mixture.
4. Grease your air fryer with a non-stick cooking spray and add the pickle slices to it. At this point you may need to work in batches.

5. Cook it for 8 to 10 minutes at a 400 degrees Fahrenheit, shaking halfway through. Repeat and cook the remaining batches if there are any left.
6. Serve and enjoy!

Nutritional Information per serving:

Calories: 160, Fat: 4g, Protein: 6g, Dietary Fiber: 2g, Carbohydrates: 30g

90. Delectable French Green Beans with Shallots and Almonds

Time: 25 minutes

Yield: 4

Ingredients:

- 1 ½ pounds of stemmed French green beans
- ½ pound of peeled, stemmed quartered shallots
- ¼ cup of lightly toasted silvered almonds
- 2 tablespoons of olive oil
- 1 tablespoon of salt
- 1 teaspoon of garlic salt
- 1 teaspoon of white pepper

Instructions:

1. Using a large pot, fill it with water and boil it under an average pressure of heat.
2. Add the green beans, a tablespoon of salt, stir for a while and cook it for 2 minutes.
3. Once done, drain it using a colander and allow it to cool off.

4. Using a large bowl, add the green beans, shallots, garlic salt, white pepper, olive oil and toss it until it is properly covered.
5. Place the green beans and shallots inside your air fryer basket and cook it for 25 minutes at a 400 degrees Fahrenheit, shaking it halfway through.
6. Then pick a large bowl, add the cooked green beans, shallots, almonds and toss it until it is properly covered.
7. Serve and enjoy!

Nutritional Information per serving:

Calories: 110, Fat: 9g, Protein: 3g, Carbohydrates: 7g, Dietary Fiber: 4g

91. Terrific Air-Fried Brussel Sprouts

Time: 10 minutes

Yield: 4

Ingredients:

- 1 ½ pounds of stemmed and cut in half brussel sprouts
- 2 tablespoons of melted butter
- 1 teaspoon of salt
- 1 teaspoon of black pepper

Instructions:

1. Preheat your air fryer to 390 degrees Fahrenheit.
2. Using a bowl, add and mix the brussel sprouts, melted butter, salt, and black pepper properly.
3. Then add the brussel sprouts and cook it for 5 minutes at a 390 degrees Fahrenheit, and shake it after 3 minutes.
4. Serve and enjoy!

Nutritional Information per serving:

Calories: 55, Fat: 0.9g, Dietary Fiber: 4.4g, Carbohydrates: 11.1g,
Protein: 4g

92. Super-Healthy Air-Fried Green Tomatoes

Time: 25 minutes

Yield: 4

Ingredients:

- 4 sliced into ¼-inch pieces green tomatoes
- 2 beaten eggs
- 2 tablespoons of milk
- 1 cup of flour
- ½ cup of cornmeal
- ½ cup of panko breadcrumbs
- 1 teaspoon of garlic powder
- 1 teaspoon of paprika
- 1 teaspoon of salt
- 1 teaspoon of black pepper

Instructions:

1. Using a bowl, add 1 cup of flour.
2. Pick a second bowl, add the eggs, milk and mix properly.
3. Using a third bowl, add the cornmeal, panko breadcrumbs, seasonings and mix properly.
4. For each tomato slice, dredge it in the flour, dip it into the egg mixture and then cover it with the cornmeal-breadcrumb mixture.
5. Grease your air fryer basket with a nonstick cooking spray.

6. Working in batches, add the green tomatoes, cook it for 20 minutes at a 360 degrees Fahrenheit of heat, and flip it after 10 minutes.
7. Repeat the above step with any leftover.
8. Serve and enjoy!

Nutritional Information per serving:

Calories: 190, Fat: 12g, Protein: 4g, Dietary Fiber: 6g, Protein: 4.25g

93. Luscious Air-Fried Broccoli Crisps

Time: 35 minutes

Yield: 4

Ingredients:

- 1 large chopped into florets broccoli head
- 2 tablespoons of olive oil
- 1 teaspoon of salt
- 1 teaspoon of black pepper

Instructions:

1. Preheat your air fryer to 360 degrees Fahrenheit.
2. Using a bowl, add and toss the broccoli florets with the olive oil, salt, and black pepper.
3. Add the broccoli florets and cook it for 12 minutes, then shake after 6 minutes.
4. Carefully remove it from your air fryer and allow it to cool off.
5. Serve and enjoy!

Nutritional Information per serving:

Calories: 120, Fat: 9g, Protein: 4.5g, Carbohydrates: 8.3g, Dietary Fiber: 4.5g

94. Palatable Vegetable Tots

Time: 15 minutes

Yield: 2

Ingredients:

- 1 peeled zucchini
- 1 peeled carrot
- 1 beaten egg
- ¼ cup of panko breadcrumbs
- ¼ cup of grated Parmesan cheese
- 1 teaspoon of salt
- 1 teaspoon of black pepper

Instructions:

1. Preheat your air fryer to 390 degrees Fahrenheit.
2. Use a grater to grate the zucchini and carrots, squeeze out any surplus water and place it into a large bowl.
3. Using a bowl, add the panko breadcrumbs, Parmesan cheese, salt, black pepper and stir properly.
4. Mold the vegetable mixture into tots and place it inside your air fryer.
5. Cook it for 10 minutes at a 390 degrees Fahrenheit or until it has a golden brown color.
6. Serve and enjoy!

Nutritional Information per serving:

Calories: 110, Fat: 4.5g, Protein: 2g, Dietary Fiber: 5g, Carbohydrates: 15g

Chapter 10: Air Fryer Desert Recipes

95. Toothsome Caramel Cheesecake

Time: 1 hour

Yield: 8

Crust Ingredients

- 2 cups of graham cracker crumbs
- ¼ cup of brown sugar
- ½ cup of melted butter

Filling Ingredients:

- 3 (8-ounce) package of softened cream cheese
- 1 cup of brown sugar
- 3 eggs
- ¾ cup of whipping cream
- ¼ cup of coffee syrup

Caramel Sauce Ingredients:

- ½ cup of butter
- 1 ¼ cup of brown sugar
- 2 tablespoons of coffee syrup
- ½ cup of whipping cream
- 1 teaspoon of salt

Instructions:

1. Preheat your air fryer to 360 degrees Fahrenheit.
2. Apply the flour to the sides and bottoms of a spring form pan.
3. Using a bowl, add and mix all the crust ingredients properly.
4. Press the crust down into the spring form pan.

5. Then using a large mixing bowl, add and beat all the filling ingredients properly.
6. Pour the filling over the crust.
7. Place it inside your air fryer and cook it for 15 minutes.
8. Reduce the heat to 320 degrees Fahrenheit and cook it for 10 more minutes.
9. Finally, reduce the heat to 300 degrees Fahrenheit and cook it for 15 minutes.
10. Then, carefully remove it from the oven and refrigerate it for 6 hours or overnight.
11. Thereafter, using a saucepan, melt the butter under an average pressure of heat.
12. Add the brown sugar, salt, coffee syrup and mix them properly.
13. Boil and cook it for 1 minute, while still stirring consistently until the brown sugar liquefies.
14. Pour in the whipping cream, turn off the heat and thereafter allow it to cool off for 10 minutes.
15. Spread the caramel sauce over the cheesecake.
16. Serve and enjoy!

Nutritional Information per serving:

Calories: 420, Fat: 25g, Protein: 5g, Dietary Fiber: 0g, Carbohydrates: 40g

96. Magnificent Mini Cherry Cheesecakes

Time: 40 minutes

Yield: 6

Cheesecake Ingredients:

- 2 (8-ounce) package of softened cream cheese

- 1/2 cup of sour cream
- ¼ cup of sugar
- 2 eggs
- 1 teaspoon of vanilla extract
- Cherry pie filling

Crust Ingredients:

- 1 cup of crushed graham crackers
- 4 tablespoons of melted unsalted butter
- 2 tablespoons of brown sugar

Instructions:

1. Preheat your air fryer to 360 degrees Fahrenheit.
2. Line the muffin cups with the parchment paper or paper liners.
3. Using a bowl, add and stir the crushed graham crackers, melted butter, and the brown sugar.
4. Divide and press the crust proportionally into each muffin tin, which at this point will require you to be working in batches.
5. Place it inside your air fryer and bake it for 5 minutes. Once done, remove and set it aside.
6. Then using a large bowl, add and mix all the cheesecake ingredients (except for cherry filling) properly.
7. Proportionally scoop the cheesecake mixture into the muffin tin.
8. Place it inside your air fryer and bake it for 15 minutes or until it is set, while avoiding it to overcook.
9. Repeat the following steps with any leftover ingredients.
10. Refrigerate the muffin tin inside your refrigerator for 6 hours or overnight.
11. Scoop the cherry pie filling on top of each cheesecake.
12. Serve and enjoy!

Nutritional Information per serving:

Calories: 120, Fat: 4g, Protein: 6g, Dietary Fiber: 0g, Carbohydrates: 14g

97. Incredible Chocolate Chip Cookies

Time: 25 minutes

Yield: 4

Ingredients:

- 1 (12-ounce) package of semisweet chocolate chips
- 1 cup of roughly chopped nuts
- 2 cups of coconut flour
- 1 egg
- 1 teaspoon of vanilla extract
- 1 cup of softened butter
- ¾ cup of brown sugar
- ¾ cup of white sugar
- ½ teaspoon of salt
- 1 teaspoon of baking soda

Instructions:

1. Preheat your air fryer to 360 degrees Fahrenheit.
2. Using a large bowl, add and mix the brown sugar, white sugar, vanilla extract, and egg.
3. Add and stir in the coconut flour, baking soda, and salt.
4. Fold in the nuts and chocolate chips.
5. Scoop the cookie dough into a baking sheet and cook it for 6 minutes at a 360 degrees Fahrenheit.
6. Thereafter, reduce the temperature to 340 degrees Fahrenheit and cook it for an additional 2 minutes or until it sets in the middle.

7. Serve and enjoy!

Nutritional Information per serving:

Calories: 170, Fat: 9g, Protein: 2.5g, Carbohydrates: 22g, Dietary Fiber: 2g

98. Marvelous Lemon Biscuits
Time: 10 minutes

Yield: 4

Ingredients:

- ½ cup of softened unsalted butter
- 5 cups of coconut flour
- 1 lemon juice and zest
- 2 cups of coconut milk
- 2 teaspoons of yeast
- ¼ cup of granulated sugar
- 1 teaspoon of salt
- 1 teaspoon of baking soda
- 1 teaspoon of baking powder

Instructions:

1. Preheat your air fryer to 360 degrees Fahrenheit.
2. Using a bowl, add and stir the coconut flour, yeast, baking soda, baking powder, salt, and granulated sugar.
3. Add and stir in the coconut milk, lemon juice, lemon zest, unsalted butter and mix it properly until it has a soft dough's texture.
4. Roll out the pastry and cut it into biscuits.

5. Place the biscuits on a baking sheet and cook it for 5 minutes at a 360 degrees Fahrenheit.
6. Remove and allow it to cool off until it is cool enough to eat.
7. Sprinkle it with an icing sugar.
8. Serve and enjoy!

Nutritional Information per serving:

Calories: 170, Fat: 7g, Protein: 2g, Carbohydrates: 26g, Dietary Fiber: 0g

99. Everyday Strawberry Cupcakes with Strawberry Butter cream

Time: 25 minutes

Yield: 16 cupcakes

Ingredients:

- ½ cup of strawberry puree
- ½ cup of finely chopped strawberries
- 1 egg
- 2 cups of coconut flour
- ¼ cup of cornstarch
- 2 teaspoons of baking powder
- 1 teaspoon of salt
- ¾ cup of softened unsalted butter
- 1 ½ cup of granulated sugar
- 3 teaspoons of vanilla extract
- 1 cup of coconut milk

Strawberry Butter cream:

- 1 cup of frozen strawberries
- 1 cup of softened unsalted butter
- 4 cups of powdered sugar
- 3 tablespoons of heavy cream
- 1 teaspoon of vanilla extract
- ½ teaspoon of salt

Instructions:

1. Preheat your air fryer to 350 degrees Fahrenheit.
2. Line a muffin cups with a parchment paper or cupcake liners. (This recipe will make around 16 cupcakes, so you will need to cook in batches.)
3. Using a large bowl, add and mix all the cupcake ingredients properly.
4. Proportionally scoop the cupcake batters into the muffin cups.
5. Place it inside your oven and cook it for 20 minutes or until a toothpick comes out clean in the center. Remove and allow it to cool off, and cook any remaining cupcakes if necessary.
6. Using a blender or food processor, add all the butter cream ingredients and blend it until it is totally grounded.
7. Scoop the butter cream into each cupcake.
8. Serve and enjoy!

Nutritional Information per serving:

Calories: 145, Fat: 5g, Protein: 1g, Carbohydrates: 35g, Dietary Fiber: 1.2g

100. Super Yummy Brownies

Time: 25 minutes

Yield: 4

Ingredients:

- 4-ounces of softened unsalted butter
- 8-ounces of bittersweet chocolate chips
- 3 eggs
- 1 cup of granulated sugar
- ½ teaspoon of salt
- 1 cup of all-purpose flour

Instructions:

1. Preheat your air fryer to 350 degrees Fahrenheit.
2. Grease a heat-safe dish that is convenient with your air fryer.
3. Using a double boiler, melt the butter and chocolate.
4. Then using a large bowl, add and mix all the ingredients properly.
5. Add the brownie batter to the greased heat-safe dish and smoothen the surface.
6. Place it in your air fryer and cook it for 25 minutes or until a toothpick comes out clean in the center.
7. Remove the brownies and allow it to chill until it is cool enough to eat, thereafter cut it into squares.
8. Serve and enjoy!

Nutritional Information per serving:

Calories: 130, Fat: 5g, Protein: 2g, Carbohydrates: 21g, Dietary Fiber: 0.6g

101. Summer Fruit Crumble Mug Cakes

Time: 30 minutes

Yield: 4

Ingredients:

- 1 cup of all-purpose flour
- ½ cup of melted butter
- ¼ cup of brown sugar
- ¼ cup of oats
- ¼ cup of granulated sugar
- 1 tablespoon of honey
- 1 cup of blueberries
- 2 cored, peeled, and finely chopped apples
- 2 cored, peeled, and finely chopped pears
- 2 cored, peeled, and finely chopped peaches

Instructions:

1. Preheat your air fryer to 320 degrees Fahrenheit.
2. Using 4 mugs, proportionally add the blueberries, apples, pears, and peaches into each and every one of them.
3. Sprinkle it with the brown sugar and honey until the fruit is completely covered.
4. Using a bowl, add and mix the flour, butter, and granulated sugar properly.
5. Add the oats and mix properly.
6. Proportionally cover each mug with the oat crumble.
7. Place it inside your air fryer and bake it for 10 minutes at a 320 degrees Fahrenheit.
8. Thereafter increase the heat to 390 degrees Fahrenheit and cook it for an additional 5 minutes.
9. Carefully remove it from your oven and allow it to cool off.
10. Serve and enjoy!

Nutritional Information per serving:

Calories: 190, Fat: 8g, Protein: 2g, Carbohydrates: 29g, Dietary Fiber: 4g

102. Satisfying Mini Pumpkin Pies

Time: 30 minutes

Yield: 6

Ingredients:

- 1 cup of canned pumpkin
- ½ cup of Original Bisquick mix
- ½ cup of sugar
- ¾ cup of evaporated milk
- 2 teaspoons of pumpkin pie spice
- 1 teaspoon of vanilla extract
- 2 eggs
- 1 cup of whipped cream (for serving)

Instructions:

1. Preheat your air fryer to 370 degrees Fahrenheit.
2. Line the muffin cups with a parchment paper or muffin liners.
3. Using a bowl, add and mix all the ingredients except for the whipped cream.
4. Proportionally scoop the pumpkin mixture into every muffin cup.
5. Place it inside your air fryer and bake it for 15 minutes.
6. Remove and allow it to cool off for 10 minutes.
7. Serve and enjoy it with a tablespoon of whipped cream!

Nutritional Information per serving:

Calories: 280, Fat: 7g, Protein: 21g, Dietary Fiber: 3g, Carbohydrates: 32g

103. Dazzling Air Fryer Berry Crumble

Time: 30 minutes

Yield: 4

Ingredients:

- ½ cup of coconut flour
- ½ cup of brown sugar
- ¾ cup of granulated sugar
- 1 teaspoon of cinnamon
- 1/8 teaspoon of salt
- ½ cup of oats
- 2 tablespoons of cornstarch
- 6 tablespoons of softened and chopped butter
- 4 cups of mixed berries

Instructions:

1. Preheat your oven to 350 degrees Fahrenheit.
2. Using a large mixing bowl, add and mix the coconut flour, brown sugar, ¼ cup of granulated sugar, cinnamon, salt, and the oats properly
3. Then pick another bowl, add and mix the 4 cups of mixed berries, ½ cup of granulated sugar, and the cornstarch.
4. Grease 4 medium ramekins with a nonstick cooking spray.
5. Add the mixed berries mixture, and top it with the crumble toppings.
6. Place it inside your air fryer and cook it for 15 minutes.
7. Carefully remove it from your air fryer and allow it to chill.
8. Serve and enjoy!

Nutritional Information per serving:

Calories: 220, Fat: 7g, Protein: 4g, Dietary Fiber: 11g, Carbohydrates: 35g

104. Heavenly Air Fryer Apple Dumplings

Time: 35 minutes

Yield: 2

Ingredients:

- 2 cored and peeled apples
- 2 tablespoons of raisins
- 1 tablespoon of brown sugar
- 2 sheets of puff pastry
- 2 tablespoons of melted butter

Instructions:

1. Preheat your air fryer to 360 degrees Fahrenheit.
2. Using a bowl, add and mix the raisins with the brown sugar.
3. Fill the apple core with the brown-sugar coated raisins.
4. Place the apple on the puffy pastry sheet and wrap until the apple is completely covered.
5. Brush the pastry sheet with the melted butter and place it inside your air fryer.
6. Cook it for 25 minutes or until it gets softened and has a golden brown color.
7. Carefully remove it from your air fryer and allow it to cool off before serving.
8. Serve and enjoy!

Nutritional Information per serving:

Calories: 410, Fat: 19g, Protein: 4g, Carbohydrates: 58g, Dietary Fiber: 0g

105. Amazingly Delicious Chocolate Cookie Dough

Time: 25 minutes

Yield: 4

Ingredients:

- ½ cup of softened butter
- 1/3 cup of brown sugar
- 1 ¼ cup of self-raising flour
- 2/3 cup of semisweet chocolate chips
- 4 tablespoons of honey
- 1 tablespoon of milk

Instructions:

1. Preheat your air fryer to 320 degrees Fahrenheit.
2. Using a large bowl, add and mix the butter and sugar properly.
3. Add and stir in the honey and flour.
4. Crush the chocolate chips into tiny pieces and stir it into the cookie dough mix.
5. Using a ladle, serve the cookie dough into a cookie tin in your air fryer that has been already covered with a baking sheet.
6. Place it inside your air fryer and cook it for 20 minutes at a 320 degrees Fahrenheit.
7. Serve and enjoy!

Nutritional Information per serving:

Calories: 260, Fat: 14g, Protein: 2g, Carbohydrates: 30g, Dietary Fiber: 4g

Conclusion

Hopefully, after going through this book and trying out a couple of recipes, you will get to understand the flexibility and utility of the air fryers. It is certainly a multipurpose kitchen appliance that is highly recommended to everybody as it presents one with a palatable atmosphere to enjoy fried foods that are not only delicious but healthy, cheaper, and more convenient. The use of this kitchen appliance ensures that the making of some of your favorite snacks and meals will be carried out in a stress free manner without hassling around, which invariably legitimizes its worth and gives you a value for your money.

This book will be your all-time guide to understanding the basics of the air fryer, because with all the recipes mentioned in the book, it is rest assured that it will be something that you and the rest of the people around the world will enjoy for the rest of your lives. Also after going through this book , you will be able to prepare delicious and flavorsome meals that will not only be easy to carry out, but tasty and healthy as well.

However, you should never limit yourself to the recipes solely mentioned in this cookbook, go on and try new things! Explore new recipes! Experiment with different ingredients, seasonings and different methods! Create some new recipes and keep your mind open. By so doing you will be able to get the best out of your air fryer.

In a nutshell, if you found this book helpful, please kindly take the time to leave an honest review on Amazon. Your feedback will be greatly appreciated. Thank you, and the best wishes to you!

CPSIA information can be obtained
at www.ICGtesting.com
Printed in the USA
BVOW09s1036171217

503035BV00012B/1133/P